the **game** of work

D1051796

the
game
of work
Charles A. Coonradt
With Lee Nelson

GIBBS SMITH
TO ENRICH AND INSPIRE HUMANKIND

©2012 Gibbs Smith, Publisher   © 2007 Charles A. Coonradt

Previously published and copyrighted:

© 1984 Liberty Press

© 1991, 1997, 1999, 2001 Charles A. Coonradt

All rights reserved. No part of this book may be reproduced by any means whatsoever without written permission from the publisher, except brief portions quoted for purpose of review.

Published by Gibbs Smith, Publisher

P.O. Box 667

Layton, Utah 84041

Orders: 1.800.835.4993

www.gibbs-smith.com

Designed by Jody Billert / Design Literate, Inc.

Printed and bound in United States

Library of Congress Cataloging-in-Publication Data

Coonradt, Charles A.

The game of work : how to enjoy work as much as play / Charles A. Coonradt, with Lee Nelson. -- 1st ed.

    p. cm.

Includes index.

ISBN-13: 978-1-4236-3085-2 (paperback)

ISBN-13: 978-1-4236-0157-9 (hardcover)

    1. Employee motivation. 2. Motivation (Psychology) 3. Work--Psychological aspects. I. Nelson, Lee. II. Title.

HF5549.5.M63C674 2007

650.1--dc22

                        2007009148

To my son Christopher, who taught us
about winning though his game was very short.

A portion of the proceeds from the sale of this book
has been donated to the Ronald McDonald House
in Christopher's memory

Contents

Foreword

Human nature is a powerful thing. Yet our lives seem to be littered with initiatives that encourage us to go against our nature—our human nature. We try to lose weight by eating the "right" foods and avoiding those foods that are not "good for you." In our elementary schools we expect a ten-year-old boy, full of energy and curiosity, to sit still for hours performing repetitive tasks. In business, we all say that our people make the difference. The strategies we pursue talk of innovation and "out-of-the-box thinking." Yet we reward predictability and those who get along.

There is a saying in Japan that "the lone nail gets hammered down." I find that to be ever so true in my twenty-five years of business experience. Seminars, workshops, on-the-job training, and countless other programs and processes are all geared toward improving our collective performance, while often pushing our individual identity further into obscurity. The net result of this process is that we begin to *view ourselves* through the lenses of what we do. Our business card soon no longer defines what we do, but *who we are.* I believe this conventional approach is the most difficult path to sustained corporate and individual performance because it conflicts with our human nature.

Nearly twenty years ago I came across Chuck Coonradt. One of the most talented managers I have ever had the pleasure to work with, Gary, encouraged me to come and see Chuck's approach firsthand. I was an executive at Pepsi-Cola at the time and in the midst of a series of bottling acquisitions throughout the West. I had assigned Gary to lead our newly acquired operations in Utah, and in a very short time I noticed that his performance clearly stood out. Though extremely competent and creative, he was also *very* cynical of consultants and other outside experts.

I met Chuck for the first time in Phoenix. I was immediately a little suspect when Gary told me that Chuck would lead off the morning session with a two-and-one-half-hour presentation. Up to that point, I had never experienced anything instructional that took over two hours that didn't bore me to death!

Let me tell you, I have never been so wrong about something in my life. For nearly three hours Chuck had me and the other forty or so people there on the edge of our chairs. Essentially in that time, through his presentation, he brought to life this book *The Game of Work.*

This book and Chuck's approach is all about making human nature work *for you,* rather than against you. The fundamental concept is simple, yet so insightful when *applied* to our everyday work life. That is, people in general would much rather play than work. I find the concepts in this book work not just in the context of business, but just as well in our day-to-day lives. It is a wonderful tool to help anyone leverage how people naturally react and behave.

Rewarding the behavior you want repeated is obvious, but we often don't do it. I have found that knowing the rules, or the *field of play*, empowers people to innovate and take risks, without worrying if they are putting their job or career at risk. People like playing games because they know the rules and the score. We play games to win. When we don't know the score or the rule, which is unfortunately the situation all too often for most people when they are at work, we tend not to want to play or we play safe.

Just think of how many companies fail because their employees are just playing safe—playing not to lose. Or even worse, how many of us have associates that show up every day, but *really* don't want to play.

This book provides simple tools that anyone can take and easily apply tomorrow to get more employees to play. It is a "quick" read unlike most business books. The concepts are simple and often analogous to the games we play as kids or adults. I also find it modular in nature, meaning I can take a chapter and apply a tool independently.

I have applied this book and its concepts for over twenty years. Thus I find that *The Game of Work* has sustained the test of time. It has been used in all types of companies in all types of environments with equal success, from small work groups to literally the largest company in the world. From the lowest level frontline associate to the most senior executive, it works. I have found it is the one concept that, even without any direct support on my part, managers within the organization independently seek Chuck's help. And for those skeptics out there (like me), I have seen this adoption process happen long after the initial sponsor has left the organization.

Life is about how we interact and motivate people, whether it's with family, friends, co-workers, or the countless others we depend on in our daily lives. Imagine if everyone we encountered was motivated and approached their work life with the enthusiasm they have for their favorite game. The fact is that most people *want* that.

Business demands measurable results. Sales, costs, return on investment, and customer service are measured by most companies in excruciating detail. Though there will always be debate about cause and effect, most business experts agree there is a positive correlation between employee engagement and results. I must admit it has been easier and more fun to drive these key business metrics with the help of a turned-on workforce. This book from the "oracle from Utah" does just that.

The Game of Work is a powerful, yet simple book that can transform any team to work with the same passion with which we play. When people work like they play, the results tend to exceed expectations. It is just human nature!

LAWRENCE V. JACKSON
JUNE 25, 2006

Acknowledgments

No great work is ever accomplished by the writer alone. Just as Plato had Aristotle, the concepts developed in the following pages are based on the efforts, at least in part, of those who have gone before. Napoleon Hill, in his book *Think and Grow Rich,* was the mentor for us all, and my involvement with Success Motivation Institute and its president, Paul J. Meyer, was a springboard for many of the concepts developed in this volume. Since 1971 his programs have had a profound impact upon my life and accomplishments. I have endeavored in this book to identify specific material borrowed from all sources and wish to express an overall appreciation to the pioneers who made it possible for books like this one to be written.

The testing, modifying, and continuing evolution of this book has been and is being done by all the members of the Game of Work. I owe special thanks to our officers and staff, for their ability to put wings on these ideas and make them fly.

Introduction

The Game of Work works. Since its first press run in 1984, *The Game of Work* has helped thousands of companies and hundreds of thousands of managers and employees experience increased job enjoyment while producing extraordinary results. It still works today.

It works because it speaks to the human need to be better—better at home, better at work, better at life in general. No one wants to be "managed," and we all want to be fulfilled. Our desire to do a job well, and to be recognized and rewarded for that job, is part of the basic human makeup. The conventional "management by exception" theory is contrary to that basic human need. When most of our people are doing their job correctly most of the time, it is inappropriate to have them receive mostly negative feedback. No news is not good news, it is simply "no news" and is too often interpreted as "bad" news.

Coach John Wooden said, "It is what we learn after we think we know it all that really matters."

What we've discovered is that human nature doesn't change and our proven methods are not trendy, or the latest management consulting style, or the latest best seller by the newest management guru. The Game of Work is not a silver bullet or a magic potion that can be swallowed or experienced in one evangelical weekend. The Game of Work requires a leader's dedication to his or her team members and a willingness to change behavior to produce better results.

Zig Ziglar said, "You can get anything you want if you help enough people get what they want." That is the bargain of life. The methodology and thought technology captured in the Game of Work gives each leader the keys to unlocking that unlimited human potential.

From baby boomers to Generation X to the Digital Generation of the twenty-first century, it is more important to find the similarities in people's job expectations and experiences than to focus on the differences.

The five principles of the Motivation of Recreation are:

- Clearly defined goals
- Better scorekeeping and scorecards
- More frequent feedback
- A higher degree of personal choice of methods
- Consistent coaching

Adventure travel is expanding each year; marathon participation is at an all-time high, with seniors as the fastest-growing segment of runners. Fantasy leagues exist in every professional sport in our country. Title IX has produced a generation of female athletes at the college level and contributed to record attendance for the LPGA and WNBA unheard of at women's sports events twenty years ago.

During the same period of time, worker satisfaction levels remained stagnant, if not slightly declining. Clearly the need to elevate our people's satisfaction with their "at-work" experience remains a challenge today as it has throughout the industrial age. The Game of Work addresses, in a fiscally responsible way, the challenge of on-the-job satisfaction.

As qualified people become increasingly difficult to attract and retain, the implementation of the five principles in this book, which creates a culture of appropriate feedback in organizations, is the one key factor to improving results, retention, and recruitment. It has long been accepted by psychologists that people stay where they are treated well and leave when they feel unwanted or underappreciated. That is true, has been true, and will always be true in marriage, family, and work.

This works because the Game of Work does not require the team to learn some new vernacular and dictionary of terms to be successful. It is written in the familiar language that we hear every day. It works because it is inclusive of all backgrounds and experience levels.

You cannot reduce manufacturing costs in a hundred-year-old consumer package-goods company by 21 percent over the prior year without gaining engagement from all of the team members. The Game of Work works because it is a process we do WITH team members not TO team members.

You cannot improve advertising effectiveness rates in a national real estate company by 400 percent until the person facilitating that program changes her perception from being "just a clerk" to understanding how she can win every day and scores that improvement.

You cannot take labor cost per piece in a large national retailer's return department down by 14 percent vs. budget (and 22 percent versus the prior year) without the engagement and the enthusiasm produced by selecting which scorecards matter and getting true team member ownership.

When a CFO in the last decade of his career and a director of marketing in her first decade of work from the same company both select scorecards that allow them to win at their jobs, and deliver double-digit improvement, I know we are touching fundamental human needs to achieve.

I believe in the human desire to succeed more strongly today than when we first published this text. Our obsession with recreational pursuits is driven by that need. We know the length of our longest hike, the time of our best marathon race, even the amount of time we take off, is a clear statistic. The competition for most of us is not against others, although that certainly plays a role when it is chosen, but rather against our own previous best.

When leaders in companies can embrace the Motivation of Recreation that produces such natural highs of engagement, enthusiasm, and energy, and bring it to their area of responsibility, then results will be there with the twenty-somethings, as well as with those in the twilight of their careers.

Why today? Because since our earliest history mankind has been committed to "better," and because the Game of Work continues to teach leaders to recognize and celebrate being better. That is the key, regardless of age and background. When we teach people how to win every day they reward us with the results we desire.

Let the games continue.

CHUCK COONRADT

·one·

The Game of Work

*People will pay for the privilege of working harder than
they will work when they are paid.*

CHUCK COONRADT

In the frozen-food business, people are hired to work in refrigerated warehouses in terrible working conditions at near-zero temperatures. But the unions and OSHA have done much to make conditions bearable. Companies are required to provide insulated clothing and boots. In fact, an entire industry provides clothing specifically for companies with refrigerated warehouses. These companies are required to provide hot drinks within so many feet of cold work areas. Workers must have a ten-minute break every hour. It's tough to get people to work in those kinds of conditions. People dislike working in the cold.

Yet whenever a winter snowstorm passes over my home in the mountains, followed by clearing skies and plunging temperatures, there is a sudden jump in employee absenteeism, particularly among young workers. Instead of staying home to avoid the freezing temperatures, they migrate up the local canyons to test the famous fresh powder snow at Alta, Snowbird, or Park City. Equipped with hundreds of dollars' worth of equipment, they gladly take a reduction in pay for the day off and buy a seventy-five-dollar pass to spend the day outside in subfreezing temperatures. There are no hot-drink vending machines on the slopes, nor have I ever heard of a skier demanding a ten-minute break every hour. People really will pay for the privilege of working harder than they will work when they are paid.

Consider deer hunting. Every year, during the third week in October, hundreds of thousands of men drag themselves to work Monday through Thursday. They are slow and lethargic, saving their energy for the weekend. Then on Thursday afternoon, it's as if every one of them takes some kind of magic energy pill. Their eyes open wide. They stay up all night cleaning rifles, sharpening knives, waterproofing boots, and loading the camper with hundreds of dollars' worth of food. Friday morning they spend five or six hours driving along the roughest roads in the world, often in snowstorms. The next morning, the same men who on workdays have trouble fixing a bowl of cold cereal are up at 4 a.m. fixing a huge breakfast of bacon, eggs, fried potatoes, juice, and hot drinks.

After breakfast they wander out into a freezing blizzard, hoping for a chance to drag a dead deer through places they wouldn't carry their dying friend—all the time pretending the meat they might get is an economical investment to cut future grocery bills. Those hunters pay for the privilege of working harder than they will work when they are paid.

But why? Why do people put up to ten times as much energy

and effort into their avocations as into their vocations? Why will people pay for the privilege of working harder than they will work when they are paid? There are several reasons.

First, *in recreation goals are clearly defined*: shooting a deer; winning a game; beating your previous time. The desired result is clear and easily measured.

I've always wanted to play the Pebble Beach Gold Course in Carmel, California. That's where they hold the annual AT&T National Pro-Am tournament.

Let's assume I finally make it to the course.

"I'm here to play," I say. "Where is a map of the course?"

"We don't have a map of the course anymore," says the attendant at the door.

"How do I know where to play? Where's the first tee?" I ask.

"Well, we changed," she says. "With property values so high we have converted half the course into condos. As a result, we've changed the rules some. There's no longer a first tee."

"Well, do you have a second tee?"

"We don't have a second tee, either. In fact, we don't have any tees anymore."

"Uh, well, what about the greens?"

"Don't have those either."

"Are the boundaries gone too?"

"Yes, except that it's off-limits to hit a ball into somebody's yard."

"How do I play?"

"Well," she says, "we've analyzed why people play golf, and the big reason is exercise. Here's a pedometer. Go out and walk 6,700 yards wherever you wish. You won't need a caddy because you only need to take along one club. Stop and swing it whenever you wish, a minimum of seventy times or until you feel like you've had the normal amount of exercise for an eighteen-hole game of golf."

"You're kidding!" I say.

"But the activity is still the same," she continues. "You still get the exercise, you still swing the club—you can even throw one if you want to—and you don't ever have to go look for a lost ball."

Can you imagine someone actually saying that? Or can you imagine going out on the soccer field and hearing someone say, "Listen, mostly this game is running and exercise. We don't want to do all the accounting, so we just took the goals out. You can run around kicking the ball for forty-five minutes, and then we'll take a break. Then you can run around another forty-five minutes. After that you can go home and tell everyone how well you exercised."

If you took the measurements out of the New York Marathon, there is no way in the world you'd ever get twenty thousand people to stand and wait two hours on the Brooklyn Bridge in the predawn hours for a chance to run twenty-six miles.

Second, *in recreation the scorekeeping is better* because it's (1) more objective, (2) self-administered, (3) peer audited, (4) dynamic, and (5) it allows the player to compare current personal performance with past personal performance as well as with an accepted standard.

In recreation, everybody knows how to keep score. In business, however, sometimes the strokes don't count. Frequently workers don't understand the scorekeeping system. Sometimes nobody cares. All too often there is too little objectivity in business scorekeeping.

I play golf with a handicap of eighteen. If I break 85 on eighteen holes I'm in heaven. But sometimes I play with friends who claim handicaps of eight or ten. If they hit 85, they are losing and are disappointed.

In golf you get realistic feedback that you can relate to your own past performance. If you were getting feedback on your golf game comparing you to Tiger Woods, you would soon become discouraged and quit because you could never win. But accurate feedback related to your own past performance usually gives you enough positive reinforcement to make you want to keep playing, to keep improving, to beat your own past performance standards. You win frequently enough to want to keep playing.

Have you ever met a runner who couldn't tell you how fast he runs his miles? Anybody can be a jogger—just shuffle along and you've got it. But a runner must run miles in less than eight minutes. Every serious runner keeps score. If you consistently run eight-minute miles, then you really feel good about yourself if you finish a workout averaging 7:40-minute miles. And if you break seven, that's all you can talk about all day. You don't feel bad because you didn't break the four-minute mile, or because you are not running marathons in two hours. You feel great because you are measuring yourself against your own past performance and winning. If you ran your last marathon in 4:10, then you feel great when you break four hours. You don't feel let down if you didn't make 2:40. You feel like a winner because you are not comparing your performance to some unrealistic standard.

Consider a volunteer civic tennis tournament sponsored by a local television station every summer that draws 2,700 participants with only four people keeping score. In a professional golf tournament with 140 participants, there are three people keeping score, and they sit in a tent and never see a stroke. Why? Because the scorecards are self-administered and peer audited.

In recreation, the scorekeeping enables you to receive immediate and realistic feedback. You know at all times how you are doing.

Imagine that you are on the golf course playing for twenty dollars a hole. You have two holes left to play and you're behind, so you talk your opponent into pressing the bet—double the bet on the last two holes in an effort to catch up.

You step up to the tee and blast the ball over the fence. You don't have to wait until the next six-month interview with the golf pro to know you blew it. You have been keeping your own score on every hole and know exactly where you stand.

You feel bad, not because you didn't play as well as Tiger Woods or Anita Sorsenstam, but because you didn't play up to your personal expectations corresponding to your handicap.

Scorekeeping is an effective form of motivation if it is objective, self-administered, and peer audited.

Third, *in recreation feedback is more frequent.* Everyday, everybody needs to know whether they are winning or losing. What do you think would happen if the commissioner of pro football walked onto the field at the beginning of the annual Super Bowl game to determine the best football team in the world, and said to the players, "We're going to be more businesslike in our approach to football today. We're not going to keep score. The commissioners are just going to watch the game, then meet and decide which team played the best. We'll let you know what we decide within three months." The commissioner would have to run for his life!

Fortunately, in most recreational activities you don't have to depend on a boss or supervisor to tell you how you are doing. You know what the score is as the game progresses, and nobody can change that just because they don't like you. The feedback is accurate and frequent—you know where you stand every time you throw the ball. And everybody knows how to keep score.

Feedback is the breakfast of champions. People who want to get ahead, who want to win, who want to improve and get the job done—these people want feedback. If you don't think feedback is important, go count the mirrors in your house.

If you want to improve the quality of performance in any area, you simply improve or increase the frequency of feedback. If you have a problem and you are getting a quarterly report, change it to a monthly report. If that doesn't do the job, turn it into a weekly or daily report. By increasing the frequency of your feedback, you have more opportunities to catch and eliminate problems of a solvable size.

Fourth, *in recreation participants feel they have a higher degree of choice.* Think about the words that imply a lack of choice—words frequently used in business. Words like "have to," "should," "must." How many times have you heard someone say, "I have to go play tennis?"

I'm a tennis player, and I don't think golfers get much exercise. They hit the ball, get in the cart, get out of the cart, hit the ball again, and get back in the cart. Racquetballers don't think tennis players get much exercise. We stand around, only half of the serves count, and we chase the ball half of the time. Handballers say real players don't need racquets to beat up on a little bitty ball. Part of the reason for liking a recreational activity is the free choice you have in electing to do it.

Managers must ask themselves if they are using the principle of choice when giving out assignments to employees. Are people being allowed to perform in areas where they have natural interests and abilities, or is their business like the Army of old where bakers were ordered to drive trucks? When people feel that they have no choice in what they are doing, they lose their enthusiasm, and performance suffers.

Fifth, *in recreation they don't change the rules in the middle of the game.* Imagine that you are playing pool in a strange town and winning. You just put in the eight ball when somebody announces that it didn't count because you didn't say "Homer Simpson" before it went in the hole. Obviously you are upset because someone changed the rules on you. That doesn't happen in sports. If the basketball goes through the hoop, you get two points. There are also three-point baskets, but the rules for getting those baskets are set up during the off-season, never in the middle of a game. In business, however, rules are frequently changed in the middle of the game.

One time I sat down with a regional sales manager for a light-bulb manufacturer. We were talking about scorekeeping and maintaining a high motivational level among the salespeople.

"We have a good scorekeeping system," he said. "Our people get regular reports listing their point accumulations, yet the system doesn't seem to motivate our people."

"That sounds strange," I said, because it appeared to be a good scorekeeping system.

Then he said, "I guess the thing they are upset about is the Annual National Quota Adjustment."

"What?" I said.

"Annual National Quota Adjustment," he repeated matter-of-factly, as if I ought to be familiar with the term.

"Tell me about it," I said.

"If the whole company," he explained, "does 125 percent of quota, then we depreciate the value of everybody's points back down to the 100 percent level."

"It's obvious to me," I said, "that your people can't count on a stroke being a stroke. You are changing the rules in the middle of the game."

Consider a grocery store where the meat manager has just been chewed out by the store manager for not making enough money on the meat.

"We're going to fix this," says the store manager to the meat manager. "We're going to pinch every nickel and dime in this department, and we are going to start making some money!" The meat manager nods in agreement.

Mrs. Jones comes in the store an hour later with a complaint about the roast beef she bought. She goes back to the meat manager, who has just had the rules laid down about watching the pennies. The manager gives her a hard time about exchanging the roast. She gives up and goes to the store manager, who says, "No problem, Mrs. Jones. I'll take you back and explain to that meat manager of mine how we are going to have customer satisfaction around here." The store manager has changed the rules in the middle of the game.

What if they changed the rules in a football game and the referee said after a touchdown that the ball carrier got into the end zone too easily, so the touchdown would be worth only four points?

Changing the rules in the middle of the game adds to the uncertainty of the game. Good managers seek to minimize uncertainty. Workers, like athletes, perform better when they know where they stand, when they know the score. A feeling of certainty creates a sense of security about working conditions. Managers cannot eliminate all uncertainty, but by not changing the rules in the middle of the game, they can go a long way toward minimizing uncertainty.

In the workplace, when expectations are clearly defined and uncertainty is minimized, it is easier for people to have the satisfaction of meeting expectations.

What do you think happens when these five principles are applied in the working world—when we apply the motivation of recreation to work? Can you imagine the enthusiasm level in your organization being as great for the accomplishment of your goals as you get in the bowling league or the company bridge tournament?

There's a productivity crisis in America. We hear about it every day. Yet while our workers become less productive, recreational interests and abilities are growing by leaps and bounds.

If it's 100 degrees F outside and the office air conditioning goes off, soon the temperature in the office gets up to about 80 degrees. People start tugging at their collars, saying, "Boy, it's tough working in here. We'd better go home early."

We all agree that it's tough to work when the temperature gets up to 80 degrees. But the minute we step outside where it's 100 degrees, somebody says, "What do you think, golf or tennis?"

The principles that lead to motivation in recreation can be applied to business with remarkable results. In this book I will uncover and define those principles and then teach you how to apply them.

Professional athletes are paid to play. But the enthusiasm and the power of their involvement come from the elements of the game, not the amount of the paycheck. Each of us is paid to play as well. We can increase our enthusiasm, our enjoyment, and our self-fulfillment by implementing the principles of The Game of Work. In this book you will find the way to win at your personal game of work. I guarantee it.

·two·

Goals

In the absence of clearly defined goals, we are forced to concentrate on activity and ultimately become enslaved by it.

CHUCK COONRADT

Let's take a look at what goal setting does in athletics. If you took the goals out of football, what would you have? You would give the Lombardi Trophy to the team each year that racked up the most yardage—and if you took the yard markers off the field, you would have to give it to the team whose offense could stay on the field the longest. Then football would be like many businesses that use longevity as the main criteria for promotion.

If you took the goals out of basketball, you would have ten guys running up and down the floor just dribbling the ball—as we do in business sometimes, but without the ball.

If you took the goals out of hockey, you would have twelve players on the ice fighting, and some people think that would improve the sport. Everything we do in our recreational pursuits is absolutely and totally goal directed. In hunting we have the Boone and Crockett Club to record the largest, widest, and best antler spread and the highest-quality trophy taken. Thousands of work hours a week are spent updating the Major League Baseball record book.

If you took the goals out of any sport, you would remove the most significant aspect of recreational pursuits—goal setting and goal striving. There is something inherent in us to want to do things better, faster, higher, shorter, longer—and to win.

Inspired after competing alongside the world's best swimmers as a fifteen-year-old in the Sydney Olympics, American Michael Phelps set out in earnest to be the best all-around swimmer four years later in Athens. To get there, he didn't stay in the pool two and one-half hours every day—and double that on Mondays, Wednesdays, and Fridays—just to become good. He didn't do it because it was great exercise. He did it because he had a specific goal to become the best in the world. And the eight medals they hung around his neck in Athens, six of them gold, reflect that commitment. "I think that everything is possible as long as you put your mind to it and you put the work and time into it," Phelps said.

Goals are the motivating force in athletics. And in athletics, goals are more clearly defined than in business. Goals are the main reason people will pay for the privilege of working harder than they will work when they are paid.

When we walk onto the tennis court, we know the goal is to win. When we go onto a football or soccer field, we know where we have to put ourselves and what our performance has to be to score. We must have that same challenge, that same opportunity, that same motivation when we walk into the office in the morning—instead of waiting for the phone to ring or the mail to hit the desk to get things happening.

Goals in recreation are clearly defined, and as a result, motivation in recreation is at a higher level than in business. Can we bring the motivation of recreation into the workplace? Absolutely!

When the following criteria for goal setting are applied in the workplace, they can produce motivation similar to that found in recreation.

GOALS MUST BE WRITTEN

Mike Holmgren, after his Green Bay Packers won Super Bowl XXXI, said it was because they attended every practice and chalk talk and prepared for every game with well-organized and specific written goals.

People will often avoid writing goals, saying, "I don't need to write anything. I can keep my important goals in my head. I can concentrate on the things that are really meaningful in my life." But if the phone rings in the middle of that conversation and their spouse is on the other end asking them to pick up five items from the grocery store, they say, "Hold it. Let me write this down so I won't forget."

Goals that are not written are merely wishes. There is something in the act of writing a goal down that makes it real, gives it permanence, removes it from the realm of fleeting whims. Goals that are not written down are easily forgotten or changed; written goals that are reviewed regularly become reality. Unwritten goals cannot be read and reviewed. When goals are not written, the power of conditioning through repetition is lost.

I am continuously amazed how people, after paying huge fees to attend seminars on goal setting, resist writing their goals. They must think the Super Bowl champions make up their plays during their games. Ridiculous. The main difference between professional and sandlot football is the amount of written documentation of plans.

A team's goal is not just to win the championship or to be the best. Good goals are detailed and specific—yards per carry, number of offensive and defensive plays, plays per series. Goals must be broken down into a specific plan, in writing.

It is difficult to manage any major project without having specific written goals. None of us would build a $500,000 house without a set of plans from the architect. But most average workers earning $50,000 a year for ten years ($500,000) will spend it without specific goals or plans and then wonder at the end of the ten years why they have gained nothing more than the appreciation on their house. Goals must be written.

GOALS MUST BE YOUR OWN

Super Bowl rings are won by individual players. The greatest successes in sports are the result of individual commitments to personal success.

One of the greatest stories of personal persistence I know happened at the Salt Lake City Winter Olympic Games. For half of his life, American snowboard racer Chris Klug had been chasing an Olympic medal. He'd finished sixth in the previous Olympics in Japan and set himself up as the favorite four years later when the games would be held in his home country. But that was before a serious hereditary liver disease left Klug bedridden and clinging to life while waiting for a liver transplant. When the transplant finally came after waiting seventy-two days on his back in bed, he had lost thirty pounds and considerable fitness. With only eighteen months before the games, many questioned if he should even continue his Olympic quest. Klug, however, wasn't among them and resumed training with a vengeance. Just before his final race in Salt Lake the buckle broke on his boot and he repaired it with duct tape with just seconds to spare. Shrugging off that final distraction just as he had moved past the rest of the adversity that had plagued him, he rode to the most inspirational medal of the Olympics—the first transplantee medalist in history.

Peyton Manning came into the 2006–2007 NFL postseason with a tortured past in the playoffs. The veteran All-Pro quarterback had a history of coming up short in big playoff games and he was catching a lot of flak in the national press. He then proceeded to lead the Indianapolis Colts through four straight victories, culminating in a decisive 29-17 Super Bowl victory over the Chicago Bears. Why did Peyton do so well and finally shake that monkey off his back? Was it for his team and city? No question that played a part. But mostly he did it for Peyton.

Whose company do I work for? Mine. Whose boss do I work for? Mine. Whose income am I most concerned about? Mine. I, me, my, mine. Whose goals are the most important to me? Mine.

You no doubt have observed people who go through life giving just the minimum daily requirement at work, and yet when the whistle sounds, they are off to coach a Little League team, play in a bowling league, build a mountain cabin—do something that is uniquely theirs. You've noticed the transformation, the new energy, the intelligence, the creativity, the endurance, and the capacity for work. It's awesome.

Goal setting and goal striving become truly effective only when team or corporate goals become the same as personal goals—when it becomes my team or my company. If you look at the employees of the finest organizations, the ones that we admire, they talk about "my company." These employees have entrepreneurial instincts to help ensure the success of their companies because their personal goals are intertwined with the company goals.

GOALS MUST BE POSITIVE

Vince Lombardi said that the objective of the game is to win fairly, squarely, by the rules, but to win. The goal in sports is not to avoid a loss or defeat. How many times have you seen professional golfers changing their game plan to protect their lead instead of going for everything they can get, only to see the lead slip away? They get beaten because they lose the momentum of their earlier positive attack.

The batting average is an excellent example of a positive goal. Consider a perennial All-Star like Derek Jeter, who consistently bats above .300, the accepted standard of excellence for major league baseball players. Even Jeter has not been able to bat above the mystical .400 mark, the goal achieved by Ted Williams. We consider the .400 average a positive goal. We don't look at that magical mark as being wrong 60 percent of the time. In baseball we keep track of hits and home runs, not strikeouts.

The two most common goals in America are to quit smoking and to lose weight—both negative. I used to smoke—and talk about a habit reinforced by repetition. A pack a day, 365 days a year—7,300 times a year, reaching for the smokes. The problem is getting your arm to quit moving from pocket to mouth.

Rather than have the negative goal to quit smoking, someone who wants to stop must have a goal to become a nonsmoker. Nonsmokers have tremendous benefits. They get lower rates on life and car insurance. Their clothes last longer. They don't ruin furniture or carpets. Their smell is not offensive to others. They are nonsmokers, a positive thing to be.

The problem is that most people who quit smoking still see themselves as smokers on vacation or on the wagon, and it is just a matter of time until they start up again.

I once knew a young man who told me he smoked between a

pack and a half and two packs of cigarettes a day. When I said, "Oh, thirty-five cigarettes a day," he looked at me and said, "Oh, no. It couldn't possible be that many." But if a pack and a half is thirty, and two packs is forty, then somewhere between the two is thirty-five.

As he began to clearly identify the magnitude of his habit, he then started graphing and tracking his progress to smoke a predetermined number of cigarettes a day.

The first day, I suggested that he smoke thirty-five, his average in the past and something that wouldn't present any challenge. He called me at ten o'clock that night asking, "Do I have to smoke all thirty-five? I'm up to thirty-two, and, frankly, I've had enough." To make him successful in his attempt to reach a predetermined goal, I insisted he smoke all thirty-five, which he did.

The next day he set a goal of thirty-four cigarettes. Now you might say, "Ah, clever, you're asking him to cut back a cigarette a day." No, I'm asking him to smoke a predetermined number of cigarettes each day so he can get it into his mind that he can determine in his own mind how many he will smoke every day. With that positive attitude and conditioning, his goal went to thirty-two a day, thirty-one, and thirty.

After two weeks he said he wanted to quit, but I said no, because I knew he needed more reinforcement before he stopped something he had been doing almost thirteen thousand times a year for many years. Every morning as he decided how many cigarettes and at which times he would smoke, he always kept the after-dinner smoke at the end of his list. He learned to smoke as many cigarettes as he decided each morning. When his goal finally was to smoke zero cigarettes a day, he could truly in his own mind say, "I am a nonsmoker."

The same principle applies to losing weight. Imagine losing twenty pounds. What are you going to do? Cut off an arm?

Sometimes many of us feel that would be less painful than the way we go about it. Instead of a negative goal in pounds that need to be lost, the goal must be to achieve an optimal weight and to maintain that weight once it is achieved.

The problem people have with losing weight is that after they take it off they go out and celebrate by stuffing it back on again with hot-fudge sundaes and lemon meringue pies—at least those are my favorites. You must be able to visualize the goal, and the only way the goal can be visual is if it is positive.

In basketball and football they count the points you score, not the ones you miss. But in life many times we will do 80 percent of the task and then when asked to report on it say, "Nope, I failed."

We must be willing, as the old song says, to accentuate the positive. The mind rejects negative goals; they are hard to visualize.

GOALS MUST BE MEASURABLE AND SPECIFIC

In sports we demand numbers—two, three, and even four places to the right of the decimal point. Strokes in golf are no longer a small enough measurement. It's hundredths of strokes that count. The times of swimmers, speed skaters, and downhill skiers are all measured in thousandths of seconds, and in order to separate one athlete from the others these kinds of exact measurements are essential.

How much, how many, and by when? If you can't measure it, how will you know when you achieved it? Even intangible goals need tangible indicators. If you have a goal to be more patient, count how many times you raise your voice in a day. If the numbers drop, your patience is increasing. If you are a outside salesperson, don't say, "I am going to do better next year," but "I am going to make X number of calls a day next year."

Paul J. Meyer insists, "Definite goals produce definite results. On the other hand, indefinite goals do not produce indefinite results.

1000 copies / month
$10,000
month profit

make book goal SMART
write a healthy living book
sells 100 copies month
making profit $1000/month

They produce no results at all."

If you put one hundred people in a room and ask them how many would like to be financially independent, all the hands will go up. If you then ask how many have a personal financial statement detailing assets, liabilities, and net worth that is current in the last ninety days—and I don't mean the paper they had to fill out to get a loan at the bank—ninety of those hundred people will not raise their hands.

If you ask those remaining ten people how many have that financial statement laid out in a pro-forma goals format for one-, three-, five-, ten-, and twenty-year periods, nine of the people will sit down. The one still standing will be a millionaire. It doesn't make any difference what the person's background is, how much money the person has, or what the person's current income is. That person has a plan, and because of that, you cannot turn the person aside. Goals must answer the questions how much, how many, and by when.

If your company philosophy claims that the customer is king, then you may want to measure the percentage of orders coming from repeat customers, the size of orders per customer, or the number of complaints per thousand transactions and how you dealt with them. Unless the overall goals of the company reflect how much, how many, by when, and by whom, you don't really have legitimate goals.

GOALS ARE BEST STATED IN INFLATION-PROOF TERMS

We've discussed that the elusive goal of a .400 batting average is an inflation-proof goal that has not changed in sixty-five years since Ted Williams achieved it. Salaries and commissions may go up or down. Ticket prices may go up, but some things are always the same—minutes, hours, pounds, hits, baskets, touchdowns. Goals are best stated in units of measurement that don't change.

There is a paper company in the Northwest that decided to

produce fine paper. They had already been in the pulp business for many years, and they were accustomed to measuring production in tons, not dollars. They took a controller out of headquarters and sent her over to run the new division. She was tonnage oriented, not dollar oriented, when it came to measuring production. She was told that in the fine-paper industry everything was measured in dollar value. She said, "No, we're going to count pounds and tons, even in the sales department." About this time, a sudden paper shortage appeared worldwide, and paper prices increased dramatically. While everyone else was measuring dollar sales volumes and patting themselves on the backs with 13 and 14 percent sales increases each year when prices were going up 20 and 30 percent a year, the workers at this new fine-paper division were hustling to beat pound quotas. While inflation lulled the bulk of the fine-paper companies into a false sense of security, this company was capturing a huge share of the market. They'd set their goals in noninflationary numbers.

The majority of retail stores in the United States today have not managed to have their sales per customer keep up with the increases in inflation. The actual tonnage or amount of product sold in these stores has actually decreased while dollar sales have increased. Most of them have actually been behind on the scoreboard and didn't even know it, thanks to inflation and shortsighted management. Inflation is a fact. It can be good or bad, but it is a real force in business. Only when we can take it out of our goals program, as that paper company did, can we be the beneficiaries rather than the victims of inflation.

GOALS MUST BE STATED IN THE MOST VISIBLE TERMS AVAILABLE

When goals are measured in real things, everybody knows the score. When the points go up on an NFL scoreboard, everybody knows what is happening, who is ahead, and who is catching up or widening their lead.

Goals must be measured in something you can see. Percentages are too vague. The sales representative may say to the sales manager after a long period of thought and soul-searching, "My goal is to increase my volume by 25 percent."

"Great," responds the sales manager. "According to my records, last January you achieved 10,000 unit sales. According to your goal you'll get 12,500 this January. Fantastic!"

"Wait a minute," says the sales rep. "There's no way I'll get 12,500 in January, but the 25 percent increase will be a cinch."

Nonsense. The person may have a nebulous feeling that somehow the sales can be made up in December, but that won't happen if he or she is afraid in January to face the goal in real numbers. Even dollars are better than percentages. Goals must be stated in pounds, units, calls, boxes—things you can see and touch.

Organizations can measure labor in at least four different ways:
1. Labor costs in relation to dollar sales (Most accountants prefer this measurement)
2. Dollar sales per person-hour
3. Invoices or customers served per person-hour
4. Pounds or tons produced per person-hour

The costs of both labor and dollar sales are inflationary indicators and therefore can get very complicated and hard to figure. If wage costs and sales prices do not change in a parallel fashion, you end up comparing apples to oranges. In comparing labor costs to dollar sales you are using two variables, both of which are subject to inflationary changes. You are better off comparing dollar sales to person-hours so only the first variable is vulnerable to change due to inflation. Hours are easy to measure because they are noninflationary: there will never be more than sixty minutes in an hour. Other noninflationary variable units include invoices, customers, pounds, and tons.

I once asked a group of managers how many hours a week a store would have to cut out to have a 1 percent labor savings if it had labor costs of $10,000 a week and paid its employees five dollars an hour. The responses were incredible. One manager asked me for a calculator. Another said I hadn't given enough information to solve the problem. Another asked what kind of business it was. None could quickly come up with what seemed to be a very simple answer. One percent of $10,000 is one hundred dollars. At five dollars an hour, to save one hundred dollars in a week the company would have to drop twenty hours from the schedule.

But managers shouldn't have to translate even simple problems like this one. In the heat of competition, communications have to be direct and simple, like the bidding at a bridge tournament.

In the fast-food restaurant industry, one of our clients came up with a "customers served per person-hour" measurement. It was easy to measure the number of customers per hour and at the same time know how many employees were on duty. At the end of each day the manager figured the customers served per person-hour, and future work schedules were planned accordingly.

The point is that labor-control goals are best accomplished by using specific, easily measured quantities. Managers don't have to translate. Audibles cannot be called at the line of scrimmage, as is sometimes necessary, unless everyone has been told their meaning before the game begins.

GOALS MUST CONTAIN A DEADLINE

One of my favorite examples is the 2007 Fiesta Bowl game between Oklahoma and Boise State University. With seven seconds remaining in regulation, Oklahoma was ahead 35-28 and it appeared certain that the Cinderella season of Boise State, which came into the game as the only undefeated team in the country at 12-0, was over. Boise had the ball at the fifty-yard line facing fourth-and-eighteen. There was time for just one more play.

Even when Boise State quarterback Jared Zabransky completed a twelve-yard pass to Drisan James it looked like Boise was out of luck, but then James lateraled to teammate Jerard Rabb, who didn't stop running until he was in the end zone with a game-tying touchdown.

In the resulting overtime, Oklahoma took the lead again on a touchdown and point-after kick, 42-35. But by now Boise was used to operating with its back against the wall. On fourth down and goal to go—another do-or-lose situation—the ball was hiked directly to Boise running back Vinny Perretta, who threw a touchdown pass to Derek Schouman, making the score 42-41. Electing to try for the win by going for a two-point conversion, the Broncos' Zabransky cocked back his arm as if to pass and Ian Johnson took the ball out of his hand and ran into the end zone in a perfectly executed Statue of Liberty play. Faced three times with extinction, the Boise State Broncos brought out three trick plays they had reserved for just such a situation to save the day. Theirs may be the most improbable triumph in major college football bowl history.

If you don't have a deadline, you don't have a goal. Goals must say how much, how many, and by when.

The most exciting play in all of sports occurs in those last two minutes before the half, or the last two minutes before the end of any given period, whether it is a hockey, basketball, or football game.

Deadlines allow the student who has slept in all term, not able to get out of bed before 10 a.m., to stay up all night studying for a midterm exam. Deadlines account for 40 percent of the money raised in any telethon to be raised during the last 20 percent of the time. Deadlines are covered in one of Murphy's Laws that says, "The first 10 percent of a project requires 90 percent of the time allowed for the entire project to be completed. The second 90 percent requires 90 percent of the time allowed for it, and that's why it takes twice as long as it should."

Deadlines are the foundation of commitment. Deadlines are the adrenaline boosters. Deadlines are the instigators of achievement and inventiveness. A goal without a deadline is merely a philosophical statement.

GOALS MUST ALLOW FOR PERSONALITY CHANGES

In 1995, Derek Parra was the best inline skater in the world, with eighteen world titles to his credit and a projection of many more to come. He was the king of his domain. But there was a problem. Inline skating isn't included in the Olympics and Parra dreamed of winning an Olympic gold medal. So at the age of twenty-five he switched to the sport of speedskating, a cousin of inline skating but with two important differences: you race on skates instead of wheels and on ice instead of asphalt.

There was nothing easy about the switch. Parra had grown up in southern California and had barely ever seen any ice, let alone spent any time on it. Overnight, he went from being No. 1 in the world to just somebody in the back of the pack. But he stuck to his goals and persisted in making the transition and by the 2002 Winter Olympic Games in Salt Lake City he won his Olympic gold medal.

You must change, too, like starting to get up at 6 a.m., working a full day, cutting out the long lunches.

If you double your income next year, how will you spend it? Where will you put it? Unless you've got someplace for it to go, there's no reason to do it or make it. The reason most of us don't make more money than we do right now is because we don't know what we'd do if we had it. It sounds odd, but it's true.

J. Paul Getty wrote a book called *Being Rich*. Not Getting Rich, but *Being Rich*. He talked about the responsibilities of wealth and the personality traits necessary to develop and manage wealth. Paul J. Meyer said, "You must first set goals to become before you attempt to set goals to have."

The goals to become are the intangible characteristics that make winners what they are. You cannot, for example, become a great skier if you have a strong fear of injury.

If you take average people in an average job earning an average income, you can guess that they will probably never get ahead as long as things stay the same. But if they find themselves in a traumatic situation, maybe a costly divorce, a major operation without insurance to cover the costs, any financially taxing situation, then they will rise to the increased need and generate an increased income. Or they might fall back into the role of a loser and look to someone else, or the government, to meet their obligations. But we can and do change with goals or traumatic experiences. Winners are champions of change and choice.

GOALS MUST CONTAIN AN INTERRELATED STATEMENT OF BENEFITS

Goals and benefits go together. The acronym WIIFM stands for, "What's in it for me?" Make sure you've got some WIIFM in your goals program.

There is no question that Olympic athletes are motivated by the thrill of the chase, honor of country, and the desire to stand on that medal podium at the highest level. But all of us know that the gold translates into "green" in the form of contracts for endorsements, appearances, and products. One of the great benefits of our capitalistic system is the opportunity to keep the WIIFM in all we do.

When I turn in my sales goal, I translate the bottom line into dollars, break it down into a budget (what I will need to live on), and then decide what I want to do with the rest of it.

When preparing your goals, take out a chunk of money just for you after all the living expenses are covered. If it isn't big enough, and you're a salesperson, go back to the sales manager and ask for permission to raise your goal.

WIIFM explains the *why* to people. Everybody, when asked to do something unusual or out of the ordinary, wants to know *why*. They are not as interested in the *how*. Our communication won't be very effective if we are trying to shove the *how* down someone's throat when he or she is still waiting to hear the *why*. But if we can clearly define the *why*, then we will have the kind of performance we want and the *how* will pretty much take care of itself.

Too often we think our communications are not being received or that people are resistant to our requests. This happens most when we are trying to insist on a course of action when they still don't understand *why* it's important. The great paradox is that when something didn't get done, we go back and ask, "*Why* didn't you do it?"

The *why* in sports is apparent. You wouldn't think of going on a basketball court except to win. You wouldn't think of being in a race unless it was to win or to get a better time. You wouldn't think of going hunting unless you hoped to come home with something other than sore feet. The *why* is such an integral part of recreation that we sometimes overlook its significance. The *why* also needs to be in personal, business, and volunteer activities. Any goal without a benefit statement has no motivational value. Goals must be realistic and obtainable, and they must also carry a promise of reward if achieved.

A good idea in setting goals is to establish a tangible reward for yourself when the goal is accomplished. All of us go through life spending money—house payment, groceries, utilities, car payments, clothing. How exciting. When was the last time you told your spouse you couldn't wait to finish dinner so you could sit down at the desk and pay the gas bill?

There's nothing inherently exciting about going out to buy a new business wardrobe. But it can be exciting if it's a reward for reaching a goal. I'd rather buy a suit as a reward for accomplishing something important to me than because the store puts them on sale. I might pay a little more, but every time I put on that suit the success I enjoyed in reaching the goal will be reinforced. When you have a tangible reward, reaching a goal becomes a *want to* instead of a *have to* experience, and that makes a big difference.

If you enjoy great music, go out and buy yourself a favorite CD after reaching a goal. Write on the cover why you bought it. When you get down in the dumps and can't get yourself going, get out your recordings and listen to them. While you're listening, read what you have written on the covers and remember how you achieved those goals. You won't be down in the dumps after half an hour or half a day of that kind of conditioning. The good get better when they celebrate their victories. And if you have tangible memories of your victories you won't forget them.

GOALS MUST BE REALISTIC AND OBTAINABLE

In football, goals are usually made by a yard here, a yard there. Woody Hayes, one of the great legends in college football, is famous for the phrase "three yards and a cloud of dust." With that concept Woody dominated Big 10 football for decades. The three-yards-and-a-cloud-of-dust attitude will get you farther than any instant accomplishment or get-rich-quick scheme.

If you've never earned very much over $50,000 a year and you've established that as your average for a long time, don't suddenly decide that overnight your earning level will jump to

$100,000. Most of us are not capable of making the personality and the work-habit changes necessary to have such a sudden change in earning ability. But if you set realistic goals and work on them and work on them and work on them, you can get big results. It's like those IRA advertisements. They say if you start making small deposits at age twenty-five and stick with it, you will be a millionaire by the time you retire. Paul J. Meyer calls that progressive realization. I call it the secret of success. There are a million dollars in your head, if you can just figure out how to get them out. Keep after it.

Generally, reading a self-help book or taking a motivation course produces little real change. Change is hard to achieve, frequently like that final yard into the end zone in a championship game. But the more realistic and attainable your goals are, the greater your chance of seeing some change, at least a little.

Every company must have overall organizational goals, followed by divisional and departmental ones, and then the individual goals of each member of the organization. All those goals must work together.

Sometimes when companies get down to the departmental goals, they think that is where goal setting stops. Supervisors are told not to interfere with the private goals of individuals, not to get too close. That's bunk. *Individual goals are the foundation of corporate human-resource development and planning.*

Individuals are motivated by needs and wants. An organization that not only understands the needs and wants of its workers but to a certain degree even influences those wants will be better able to get maximum productivity out of those workers.

Many of us are trained from early childhood not to want. Maybe a well-meaning Sunday School teacher implied that we cannot be rich and righteous at the same time. But we cannot increase our motivation until we increase our desires. Having goals means having desires.

The clear definition of individual goals is the foundation of teamwork. One time an NBA team lost its all-pro point guard at the beginning of the semifinal playoff series. The other starters changed their play to compensate for the loss of the guard, and the team lost the first three games. It wasn't until the coach put in the backup point guard and told the team to play as if the star was in, that the team finally came together and pushed the series to seven games. *Teamwork is based on great individual execution.*

·three·

Scorekeeping

If you can't measure it, you can't manage it.
George Odiorne

Have you ever noticed the difference between figure-skating and ice-hockey crowds? The figure-skating crowd offers polite applause when they see a good skating exhibition. The ice-hockey fans scream and yell when they see something they like, or don't like, on the ice. What's the difference? Both sports take place on the ice and both involve skilled skaters who have spent many years preparing to perform.

One reason figure-skating crowds are so timid is that they don't know for sure what is happening on the ice. They know that someone is skating, but they don't know the score. After the skating is over, the judges flip up their cards—5.7, 5.6, 5.2, 6.0. It is such a bad system that they throw out the high and low scores. And the skater doesn't know if he's ahead or behind until it's too late to do anything about it. It's a terrible scorekeeping system, but until something better comes along, we'll have to live with it.

Ice hockey is different. Every fan and every player knows the score at all times. The team that is ahead knows it and takes appropriate action to protect that lead. The team that's behind knows the score too and can take catch-up action. The fans know the score and can cheer their team to victory.

Scorekeeping is the heart of athletics, and it must be the heart of every successful business. What is the first thing news reports mention about any sporting event? The score, of course! People not only want to know who won but by how much. Then come the stats, the specific measurements of individual and team accomplishments. In sports, we start with the scoreboard page and add the editorial comment. Too often in business we get this reversed.

In sports, especially professional sports, measurements are continually added to increase interest in the game. Baseball has added what they call the slugging percentage, in addition to the batting average and runs batted in. Golf has added driving accuracy, putting percentages, number of greens hit, and putts per round. Some basketball coaches are monitoring points per possession in an effort to measure the effectiveness of both offensive and defensive strategies.

Every sport has its scorecards, scoreboards, and stat sheets— and so must every business. Business managers must be on constant lookout for new measurements to improve productivity.

The primary responsibility of managers is to set the rules and create the scorecards. Archaic scorekeeping systems, or no systems at all, force employees to wait, wait, and wait for feedback from management, thinking, "I won't venture beyond where I am until I know how well I did."

Sometimes I am asked how soon scorecards should be set up for new employees. I tell them about Little League baseball. The first day the kids put on the uniform, they start tracking their batting average. They track every hitter and every fielder from the minute they step onto the field. Yet in business we frequently tell new employees to sit around for ninety days and then we'll get back to them. Too often all we measure is how they wear their hair, what they eat for lunch, or what time they like to go home. Tracking or score-keeping must begin on day one.

THREE MANAGEMENT METHODS

There are three ways to manage a company—by observation, by judgment, or by measurement. When we manage by measurement, we keep score.

Observation management

Observation management occurs when John, the sales manager, comes back from a tough sales appointment to find two of his sales representatives sitting on the table in the salesroom laughing and having a generally good time. What John doesn't know is that one of them has just lined up appointments with the executive officers of two companies John has been chasing for four years.

John has just been blown out on a sales presentation and he's not in a very good mood. As he walks by the salesroom he leans in and says, "Listen, if you two would get to work we wouldn't be in this sales slump."

Situations like that occur in companies all the time.

There are three basic problems with management by observation:

1. It is almost always inaccurate, like trying to judge a book by the cover, or a movie by the preview.

2. It is not relevant to what is going on. John observed two people sitting on a table having a good time. You can't capture all of the events in a single frame. It's like the cheerleader yelling at the referee for making the wrong call while the cheerleader's back was turned.

3. It is generally negative. There seems to be something in human nature that makes it easier to observe the negative than the positive. Had the two young salespeople been on the phone, John probably wouldn't have said anything. There's no way to win when you use observation management.

Management by judgment

Management by judgment occurs when John walks by the salesroom a second time and the two salespeople are still sitting on the table gabbing. John is likely to make a judgment: "Kids today don't work as hard as I did when I broke into the business."

In some corporations you hear the nautical phrase, "He can't get rid of his barnacles." That means the person made a mistake back in 2001 and everybody remembers it. Every time he looks as if he is getting close to that same kind of decision, they say, "Oh, yeah, you remember when he did that back in . . ." The danger with management by judgment is that too often generalizations are made from insufficient data.

When you have to correct someone, always be ultra-specific. Say, "You were forty-five minutes late for that Tuesday afternoon appointment," rather than "How come you are always late?" Unfortunately most managers manage by judgment and observation rather than by measurement. Judgment leads to prejudgment, which leads to prejudice. Prejudice leads to blindness.

Too often people make negative generalizations—that's when somebody says on Monday morning that the economy is in tough shape and nobody is buying that day. Too often businesspeople let their thoughts about one or two negative events grow like a cancer.

"You always . . ."

"You never have . . ."

"You won't . . ."

Never make a negative generalization! Even if you think it is true, it will do more harm than good. Instead, when describing a negative situation be ultra-specific. How much are sales down? How many calls did not get made? What specific behavior is it that you are concerned about? Don't make wandering generalities.

Management by measurement

Management by measurement is the one management method that works. I believe that our progress in business, or life, relates directly to our ability to measure. Four hundred years ago the most portable mechanical timepiece you could have was a water clock on a wagon. It was ten feet high and weighed three hundred pounds, and you had to pull it around with horses. And it didn't keep good time if the water slopped around. The smallest unit of distance measurement at that time was the distance from King Henry's thumb to his nose, a meter. Everything people built was designed around that unit of measurement.

Today we are much better at measuring things. We have memory chips and integrated circuits. Thousands of numbers can be sorted on a surface no larger than a pinhead. Without measuring and counting, such technology would not be possible. Quartz watches are all based on the frequency at which the quartz crystal vibrates. Our progress is based on our ability to improve measurement.

Management by measurement is relevant to the process being measured. The ability to sit on a table and carry on a friendly conversation with another salesperson is not relevant to sales success, though too much time sitting can certainly take time away from more productive activities.

So, *first, measurement is relevant to the process.* It tells you what happened, especially on the bottom line.

Second, measurement is usually exact. By that I mean when you measure something, you get the real numbers. You know where you stand. For example, if I asked you to sit down and create a financial statement, listing all your assets and liabilities, in most cases you'd discover you are better off financially than you thought you were. You are always better off when you know where you stand.

Third, exact measurements make work as enjoyable as play because participants have a way to win. When specific measurements are employed, it suddenly becomes possible for the employee to win.

You may be asking, if there are so many obvious benefits to maintaining exact measurements, why then is not more measuring going on? Perhaps some people think it is just too much trouble, or that it is too time consuming. Others may be afraid of the truth—suspecting they may not be doing a very good job. They don't think they are winning, so they don't want to know the score. What they don't realize is that they cannot win unless they keep score. There is no way to win without a score.

There are three kinds of workers or players.

1. Those who know they are winning.
2. Those who know they are losing.
3. Those who don't know the score.

It is a fact of life that those who keep score, whether they are winning or losing, win more over the long run. These are the people who accept personal responsibility for their own actions. They would rather know the score while losing than not know the score. The people who achieve financial independence do so by knowing the score. They are the people who set specific goals and keep track of progress toward those goals, even when things are not going smoothly.

I have never met a winner who didn't know the score. I have never met a professional golfer who didn't know who else was on the leader board. People play and modify their behavior based on the feedback of their progress against an acceptable standard—the scorecard.

The great tradition of Notre Dame football is reflected in a subtle fashion in the locker room; you can't help but notice all the scores of the great Notre Dame victories over their great rivals emblazoned on those walls. The impact is awesome. *Winners keep track of results. Losers keep track of reasons.*

Observers of Lance Armstrong's seven straight Tour de France victories were constantly amazed at Armstrong's attention to detail. As part of a crowded peloton of a hundred riders in a 2,000-mile, three-week bike race, Armstrong always knew not just exactly where he stood in relation to every other rider but where every one of the other riders stood as well.

He refused to leave anything to chance. The selection of his teammates. The strengths and weaknesses of his rivals. The components on his bicycle. The races he would compete in as tune-ups to the Tour. All were carefully plotted and planned. On race days, he stayed in constant radio contact with the team manager in the support car. If it was about to rain, Armstrong knew about it without having to look up. If there was oil on the road ahead, Armstrong was aware of the danger before he got there. If a rival looked strong or faltering, he knew. Other riders, not as focused, might be surprised by changing conditions and the actions of their rivals, but Armstrong was rarely surprised, and that included every year at the conclusion of the three-week race when he wore the winner's yellow jersey down the Champs-Elysees.

Winners like Lance Armstrong understand that the joy in victory is enhanced by an awareness of all the things that could defeat you.

You cannot sit by as a spectator in the game of work. You must trade your season tickets for a pair of shoes and come down on the field, the only place where points can be scored.

Management by measurement is facing the truth, taking away the language and thinking of noncommitment. When you ask people if they have completed their work yet, and they say, "Basically," "Pretty much," or "Just about," that means they have accomplished somewhere around 20 percent of the goal. These verbal diversions are a way to run away from the truth. English teachers call them euphemisms.

Euphemisms, or escape words, are rampant in business. We use the phrase "pretty much" when we have no idea at all—"pretty close" when we haven't even started. When we haven't finished a job, we say we're "just about done." *Avoiding* euphemisms vastly improves the level of communication.

There is too much truth in exact measurement for some people. Losers don't have the courage to face the truth of exact measurement. They want to run away from the truth by focusing on activities instead of results. When exact measurements are made, things are brought into clear focus, and there is no place to hide.

If you have the courage to keep score, even when you are losing, you will win more in the long run. The elimination of uncertainty through scorekeeping increases the ability to take calculated risks.

THE CASH-FLOW EUPHEMISM

One of the greatest rituals in America today takes place in the private clubs where business leaders meet to eat, exercise, and share problems with each other. When you walk into your club, somebody is likely to say, "How's business?"

You might respond, "Not bad. I just have a little cash-flow problem."

The person that asks the question, and everybody else, nod their heads knowingly like the great gods of Egypt and say, "Boy, we sure know what you mean. We're in the same situation."

What are these people saying? How can the problem not be bad if the cash won't flow, not even dribble a bit?

The *cash-flow problem* is a euphemism, a form of escapism, a way to avoid a serious business problem. *Cash flow is the barometer of business health.* Saying everything is fine except for cash flow is like saying the patient is fine except for a 105-degree temperature. Executives have to pull their heads out of the sand to face their problems and deal with them.

There's no such thing as a cash-flow problem. Cash-flow problems, as people call them, are symptoms of deeper problems. Maybe the problem is not being able to collect the money owed you. It may be that you purchased too much inventory, or the wrong kind of inventory, and don't have the courage to liquidate the excess. Maybe you don't have the courage to raise prices and go out and sell value. Or you don't have the backbone to cut unnecessary overhead—you think you can't cut anybody back even though you have enough help to do 50 percent more business. Perhaps you are bleeding the business by taking more out of the business than it is earning.

On the other hand, imagine a CEO walking into the athletic club and someone asking, "How's it going?" He responds with, "Well, not too bad, except I've bought more inventory than I know what to do with. I'm afraid to collect what people owe me. I don't have the courage to raise prices and sell on value. I'm afraid to lay off some of the employees I don't need. I'm bleeding the business by taking out more money than it is earning. But basically, things aren't bad." Everybody in the club would look at him and think, "What a uniquely truthful manager he is!"

Hitler's propaganda minister, Joseph Goebbels, said that if a lie is repeated long enough and loud enough everybody will believe it. That's the way it is with cash flow. If we are smart, we will look past the cash-flow generality to the specific places where our cash flew when we thought it was going to flow.

Cash-flow problems originate from five major problems:

1. *Too much inventory and other nonliquid assets.* Inventory is not being turned over fast enough to justify the cost of holding and handling it.

2. *Overly high receivables.* Receivables are not being collected fast enough. Perhaps credit policies have remained weak as we have moved into a time of tight cash. Our courage to collect is being dampened by our concern for additional business. Maybe we are operating on the false assumption that sales from people who won't pay are somehow beneficial to our company.

3. *Inadequate gross-profit percentages.* We are unwilling to demand the markup necessary to survive and even prosper when sales are down.

4. *Unwillingness to implement cost-cutting measures.* I never cease to be amazed at the number of people who think they can increase sales from, say, $5 to $7 million without increasing costs, and if sales drop from $5 to $3 million, who don't think they can decrease costs. When they started their business, sales were at $2 or $3 million with proportionate costs, but they think there is no way they can cut costs back when sales go into a slump.

I acknowledge the fact that some costs are irreversible without doing long-term damage to the organization—space, buildings, real estate—solidly fixed things that have ongoing costs. But it is imperative that we recognize that a building too full of people and inventory can unnecessarily drain off a lot of cash. The goal is to find that optimum level of operation where we can achieve maximum profitability and productivity. We've got to be able to bite the bullet.

5. *Inappropriate compensation for the owner or key decision-makers.* Owners or managers who combine a decrease in profitability with an increase in personal compensation are contributing to their own demise. Good farmers don't eat the seed corn.

Too often in business we forget a valuable lesson learned so well on the athletic field—that we don't negotiate the value of points. When a team scores a touchdown on an interception or fluke play, we don't run over to the field judge and say, "That one is worth only four points." No, the team gets six points, regardless of how easy the touchdown might have been. Yet in business, too often we try to mask the truth with words. We need to return to a communication style that says, "They messed up," not "Their performance is substandard, a little below the absolute minimum required in order to identify and get the job done." We have to have the courage to communicate accurately, to get to the bottom line.

We have enjoyed the comfortable euphemism of "cash-flow problems" long enough. If your cash flow has dried up—if it is simply a drip where it used to be a gusher—then look along the pipeline for the holes. Don't be content with the wandering generality that growth, that benevolent dragon, kindly gobbled up your cash and stripped away the profits. Growth is no good unless it is profitable and funded from earnings. Legitimate earnings always were and always will be the best indication of a healthy company.

Remember, there is no such thing as a cash-flow problem by itself. A shortage of cash is the result of other problems that you can do something about by keeping score.

SCOREKEEPING BASICS

Following are some of the basics of good scorekeeping.

1. *Scorekeeping must be simple and objective.* One beautiful day as I was approaching the eighteenth hole, a golfer hit a ball that bounced off a rock in a stream, hit a tree, dribbled through a sand trap, and finally rolled onto the green. The resident pro looked over at me and said, "It's a good thing the scorecard doesn't make you tell how—just how many." A basketball score doesn't tell you about lucky tip-ins or hard-fought rebounds. A football score doesn't tell you how many interceptions were made or about the dropped receptions that should have been caught. But the individual players who got the tips, blocks, interceptions, or fumble recoveries know exactly how many they got, not just for the game but for the entire season, and for last year too. Keep it simple.

2. *Scorekeeping must be self-administered.* A scorecard is most effective when it is kept and updated by the player, as in golf and tennis. That's why three people in a tent can handle all the scorekeeping responsibilities for 140 participants in a golf tournament, or why four people can handle all the record keeping for a tennis tournament with thousands of participants. Periodically managers make the mistake of having their secretaries draw all the graphs and charts, or they have computers print out the scores two or three days after the fact. Self-administered graphing and scorekeeping is best.

When people keep their own scorecards, they know whether they won or lost that day and also how much they improved, regardless of whether or not the coach had a bad day. The players will also correct any deficiencies in their scores before the cards are turned in. Our self-concept or self-image is based on what we know and can prove about ourselves. Many cross-country runners start a race with one foot forward and their right-hand fingers resting on their left wrist, ready to start their own stopwatch when the gun goes off.

3. Scorekeeping must offer a comparison between current personal performance, past personal performance, and an accepted standard. Golf wouldn't be a favorite national pastime if the only opportunity for comparison was whether we could beat the record-setting 63 Johnny Miller shot in the 1973 U.S. Open or do better than the 59s shot in competition by Annika Sorenstam and Phil Mickelson.

Golf survives and thrives because it has a scorekeeping system that allows me, for example, to compare myself, an 18 handicapper, with myself. If I go to the golf course and break 90, I get very excited. I compare my performance to my own past performance as well as to what the pros are doing.

Marathoning has a similar scorekeeping system. How many people would fight and kick and scream to get into the Boston Marathon if the clock was turned off after getting the time for the first-place finisher in each category?

The success of a scorekeeping system in recreation depends upon how well it compares current performance with past performance and with the accepted national average. Too often in business we generate a scorekeeping system that tells how well we did only in comparison to an arbitrary, artificially imposed standard.

4. Scorekeeping should be dynamic. It should allow players to review their performance during the game. In your business, is your scorekeeping more like ice hockey or figure skating? With the availability of the computer, almost every kind of business information can be immediately available. Businesses no longer have to wait until the end of the month to know how they are doing. They can know daily, even hourly. As in ice hockey, employees can know the score as the game is being played. Yet most businesses still have twelve accounting periods just like before World War II. You don't know what you did in March until the middle of April—too late to make any adjustments for March.

To sum up the principles discussed in this chapter, consider bowling-league competition. Have you ever seen a nonmotivated bowler? Everybody knows how to keep score. They throw those balls, knock down pins, and jump up and down, and you get the impression they would do almost anything for the prize money.

Work is a lot like bowling, except there's a person called a supervisor who stands in front of the pins with a curtain. The supervisor can see the pins, but the bowler can't. The bowler throws the ball, hears something, and says, "How'd I do?"

The supervisor says, "Change your grip."

The bowler says, "But how did I do?"

The supervisor says, "Move your foot." The bowler changes his grip and moves his foot and throws another ball.

The bowler hears the pins fall and asks, "How am I doing?" The supervisor says, "Put some tape in the thumb hole."

"How am I doing?" repeats the persistent bowler.

"Don't worry about it. We've got a review coming up in six months. We'll let you know then."

How long would bowling remain a popular activity under these conditions? Not very long.

Supervisors who believe in management by measurement don't hold a blanket in front of the pins while the team members are bowling. They allow the players to know exactly how many pins they knock down with each ball.

IMPLEMENTING A SCOREKEEPING SYSTEM

The measurement principles discussed in this book need to be introduced carefully into the workplace. There is almost always resistance to change, and managers or employees who in the past have focused their attention on activity can be intimidated into inactivity by the threat of disclosing performance they may feel is less than acceptable. The truth can be painful and frightening. Employees who are sold on management by measurement and want to get involved of their own free will and choice generally benefit the most from the measurement system.

Too many middle managers today feel impotent in their ability to manage, to talk, to create, to discipline, to go, to move, to build with people. Our traditional American management philosophy to manage by exception, to focus on problems, to put out fires, results in a reluctance to regularly compliment and praise. We talk about the things that are going wrong instead of the things that are going right. As a result, subordinates are depreciated with more emphasis on shortcomings than accomplishments.

A group by the name of Three Dog Night had a hit song called "Celebrate" that needs to be the theme song for managers. We have taken the emotion out of our management style. And yet we all watch the NBA champs and the winners of the Stanley Cup in the champagne showers of celebration. IBM has developed a real corporate culture around their ability to celebrate beyond expectation the accomplishment of their goals. Scorekeeping exists primarily so that we know when to begin the party.

A good scorekeeping system allows the worker or manager to establish his own self-worth in the eyes of his peers, subordinates, and supervisors. Everybody becomes more accurately and justly rewarded, stroked, or chastised, based on accurate performance records or scorecards.

·four·

Feedback

When performance is measured, performance improves.
When performance is measured and reported back, the rate
of improvement accelerates.

THOMAS S. MONSON

What do you think would happen if a head coach approached his team in the locker room before an NFL playoff game and handed the quarterback a piece of paper listing one hundred plays in sequence, saying, "These are the plays I want you guys to execute, in the exact order listed on the paper."

Do you think any of the players would object? Of course they would, all of them. They'd think the coach was insane. Why?

In order for the best possible play to be called in any given situation, it is imperative that the person calling the play have feedback from the last play, or the last several plays—how many yards gained, which lineman is getting eaten up at the line of scrimmage, direction of the wind, which receivers are being left open and which ones are getting double coverage, how many yards remain for a first down or a touchdown, and so on. All this feedback is necessary in order to make the best possible call. Handing a team a predetermined list of plays before the opening kickoff eliminates the use of feedback in calling each play as it is executed. Nobody would be surprised to find out that a team not using feedback would have trouble winning in the NFL, NCAA, or even high school.

Yet how often in business is an employee handed a job description, or a predetermined set of plays, then expected to perform without continuing feedback? It happens more often than most businesses would like to admit. Feedback is as vital in business and in life in general as in athletics.

When a spouse returns from the hair stylist and says, "How do you like my haircut?" he or she is looking for feedback. The child who has just completed a project in his or her father's shop or just finished a first attempt at mowing the lawn is always interested in an opinion from a respected peer or superior.

In athletics feedback is more clearly acknowledged and more frequent than in business. When feedback suddenly becomes available in a business situation where it has not been available before, the results can be very dramatic.

I was called in to consult with a package express company a few years ago. They were concerned, among other things, about the filing of freight bills. They are a federally controlled company, and everything has to be filed for possible audits. They file millions of items every year. Their concern was that the four people doing the filing had been three days behind for thirty-six years, the entire time the company had been in business. The day they opened the door, the filing was three days behind and they had never been able to catch up.

"If you can't measure it, you can't manage it," I said to the supervisor of the people who did the filing.

You can guess her response: "We're too busy filing them to count them."

One of the vice presidents with me suggested that the filing could be measured by weighing the stacks of material to be filed. He thought this might work because each piece was the same size and therefore the same weight. Sounded like a good idea to me, but the supervisor said, "That's the second dumb idea I've heard today."

Finally we told her we were going to try it anyway. We came up with a measurement system similar to the golf handicap. We decided to monitor ounces per person-hour.

"I don't need that stuff," said the supervisor. "My people work just as hard as anybody else in this company—all the time, every day."

"How do you know that?" I asked.

"I've got four file baskets," she said. "Every morning when I get here I spread the filing out equally into four file baskets and hand one to each file clerk, so the baskets are all even."

"What do you do on a heavy day?"

She looked at me as if I were a dummy, and she said, "Then the baskets are fuller." It was obvious at this point that this woman didn't want to be fooled with, but I persisted, telling her I wanted her to weigh the amount of filing going through the department. She didn't want to do it, but she finally agreed to weigh how much each person filed each day.

The first week we came up with an average of twenty-two ounces per person-hour. We didn't really know if that was good or bad, but it was a start. The next week we developed a scorecard for the workers and taught them how to keep score as if we were teaching them a game. They recorded their own ounces per person-hour.

An interesting thing happened. The group average for the second week increased to thirty-three ounces per person-hour. And by the end of that week they were only one day behind—the first time in thirty-six years. We were witnessing a miracle.

The supervisor came to me and said, "Listen, I can't go any faster and be accurate."

"I understand that," I said. "That's all right. Don't worry about it."

The next week production increased to forty-five ounces per person-hour. There was no monetary incentive, no threatened disciplinary measures, no promised promotions. The only difference was that they were measuring performance, keeping score. Not only was the department no longer behind, but they were finishing each day's filing by 2 p.m. By the fourth week, production had increased to fifty-four ounces per person-hour and the filing was finished each day by 11:30 a.m.

I remembered when the supervisor was doing twenty-two ounces per hour and telling me she couldn't go any faster. The last time I checked she was up to seventy-two ounces per hour and still increasing. The big payoff was that the four people doing the filing were part of an eight-person work force in that department. When two of the non-file clerks needed to quit, the file clerks came to their supervisor and said, "Listen, if you'll tell us how to measure what they've been doing, we'll just pick it up."

The executive toy mail-order catalogs sell all kinds of computerized measuring machines. A recent ad was pushing a thirty-nine-dollar pulse meter that goes on the end of your finger while you're jogging. It tells you whether you're living or dying. They've got a $199 radar gun that measures the speed of a baseball in midair. The ad says that if you measure your son or daughter's baseball pitch, the kid will learn to throw the ball faster. The same machine can be mounted on a tripod to measure your tennis serve. These machines are built and sold because the manufacturers and customers understand that when performance is measured and reported back the rate of improvement accelerates.

Probably the most significant achievement in biofeedback involves the heart. If patients can hear their heartbeat through a speaker system and see the screen on the cardiogram machine, the patients can actually learn to speed up or slow down their own heart. Feedback makes that possible.

Effective feedback is accompanied by its own set of terms, and the most important term is the *Results-to-Resources Ratio*—how much is being accomplished with the resources available—like the ounces per person-hour in the filing example. Successful managers have the capability of generating a greater result with the same amount of resources, or the same result with fewer resources. If they cannot measure it, they simply cannot do it, at least not on a regular, planned basis.

Sometimes we hear about coaches who have talented players but cannot produce a winning team. They are not able to manage their resources to produce results, and they are eventually fired.

All managers, whether they manage many people or just themselves, must make a list of all resources available to them—budget, person-hours, computer time, inventory, supplies, and so on. When you get right down to it, managers are people who turn resources into results. And the more efficiently they can do it, the more successful they are as managers. The results-to-resources ratio can be used at every level of performance.

You can only chop down a forest one tree at a time. Let the accountants figure the return on investment ratios. This book deals with the micro-measurements, like the ounces per person-hour in the filing example. When all the micro-measurements are in place, the macro-measurements will take care of themselves.

You might be thinking, "Well that was a great story about the filing company, but what I do cannot be measured like that." You'd be surprised at what can be measured, even on the human side of a business. One time I went into an organization that sold building materials. They'd been on hard times for a few years along with the rest of the building industry.

They came up with a macro problem, wanting to know what they could do about their labor costs (resource) relative to sales (result). I told them we had to find a micro-indicator measuring results to resources. It didn't have to have the same scientific accuracy the tax people demand, just something to measure change over a period of time.

First we looked at what they produced. Sales. Dollars. But who knows what's happening to the dollar with its value changing almost daily. We finally determined that we could measure the number of invoices generated by the company. Then we looked at the resource that produces invoices—person-hours.

We went back over the last eighteen months of records, including thirty-nine pay periods, and figured out the number of person-hours per invoice for each pay period. The relationship of human resource to invoice output ranged from as high as 3.7 person-hours per invoice to a low of 1.9 for a two-week pay period—a significant variation.

As we analyzed the ratios, we discovered that the 1.9 ratio occurred when business peaked during the busy summer months. The higher ratios occurred during the slow off-season. Earlier, the company had suspected they were labor heavy during the winter months, but they weren't sure how much until we started tracking the person-hours per invoice. With the confidence of exact measurement, management decided they never needed more than 2.25 person-hours per invoice, even during the slack periods.

Now, all this may not sound very sophisticated to the experienced business manager, but that company processed an average of sixteen hundred invoices per pay period. The company was able to cut out almost two thousand person-hours per pay period. So who is going to do the work? The people who are left, and they are going to do exactly what they have always done. The labor that was removed was expendable, unnecessary, but the company didn't know it until the micro-results-to-resources ratio was developed. In dealing with the human resource, managers must realize that it is flexible and can be managed to do what they want it to do. But it cannot be managed unless it is measured.

COONRADT FEEDBACK COROLLARIES

Through the years I have found two corollaries that expand on Thomas Monson's statement: "When performance is measured, performance improves. When performance is measured and reported back, the rate of improvement accelerates."

1. *Increasing the frequency of feedback improves the quality and quantity of performance.* If you're having a difficult time managing your labor resource and you're measuring it monthly, then go to a weekly measurement. It will improve. If you go to a daily measurement, it will improve again. And if you go to an hourly measurement, it may improve even more.

You may think it will take too much time to administer all these measurements. Meaningful measurement takes no time at all. In the example of the file clerks and in example after example we see that the small amount of time it takes to count results is minuscule when compared with the improved results.

2. *When feedback is illustrated on charts and graphs, the impact is even greater.* In business today we have tremendous amounts of data. It comes in stacks and boxes, making us wonder if the programmers think they are being paid for the pounds of paper they run through the printers. But data by itself is of little value. It must become useful management knowledge that can be used to make decisions. Graphs and charts make this possible by making information easier to understand and digest. In other words, the feedback—the "score"—becomes even more clear because it is graphically displayed, thus ensuring even better performance.

Remember, in the absence of clearly defined goals and accurate scorekeeping, we are forced to concentrate on activity and ultimately become enslaved by it. The goal of every business must be to get to the point where everybody on the team has an individual scorecard. Without clearly defined goals and precise scorekeeping, workers will continue to pay for the privilege of working harder than they work when they are paid.

Is timely feedback important? Is frequent feedback important? In an important match at the 2006 U.S. Tennis Open, Andre Agassi used newly developed shot-tracker technology to challenge a judge's ruling. There was a ninety-second delay as computer techs worked to bring up the image showing whether the shot was in or out. During those ninety seconds you could feel the trauma travel throughout the U.S. Tennis Center in New York and around the world through the airwaves.

What was wrong? Where was the concern? Ninety seconds, and the world was wondering if the tennis match would go on. And yet how often do we put off giving employees feedback on their performance? Do we avoid it because we don't like confrontation? Are we unwilling to sit down and explain what we need to have done, what the employees are doing right, and what they need to do to improve? Sometimes we put it off and put it off and finally walk up and say, "I've decided to give you twenty-five dollars more a week; be happy with that and go home." We need to do better than that.

If you don't think feedback is important, try telling your spouse just once that the outfit he or she has selected for a big evening is "okay."

·five·

Choice

Work consists of whatever a body is obliged to do, and play consists of whatever a body is not obliged to do.

MARK TWAIN

I'm a downhill skier. I think that walking up a mountain with a perfectly good ski lift on it is crazy, but my skinny-ski friends, the cross-country skiers, say, "Why pay somebody to haul you up a mountain that you can walk up on your own two legs?" I also think that jumping out of an airplane while the engine is still turning is absolutely crazy, but the skydivers think it's great fun; and, of course, as a certified scuba diver, I think it makes perfect sense to strap forty minutes of air on my back and then go two hundred feet from my next breath of fresh air just to get the glory of the depths. But that's choice.

Choice is what drives America. Look around your neighborhood at the various models of cars that are being driven. Look at the options. General Motors alone has over eighty models. We have over thirty different brands of skis in any length we want, manufactured all around the world. We have over sixty major golf-club manufacturers. Choice is what America is all about. It is the basis of our Declaration of Independence. It is the basis of our Constitution. We spill American blood on foreign soil in order to defend our right to vote, just so half of us can stay home every election. But if you try to take that right, that choice, away from us, we will fight to the death to retain it.

In spite of our freedom of choice, numerous surveys show that two-thirds of American workers are unhappy with their jobs. They don't always know what they would rather do, but they are unhappy with their alternatives.

Come with me at 7:30 in the morning to that major freeway leading into town. Let's post a sign that says, "If you have to go to work, turn on your lights. If you want to go to work, honk your horn." What are we going to wind up with? The quietest light show you ever saw. Come with me on that same freeway on the way home just before the Memorial Day weekend. Let's post a sign that says, "If you have to go boating, turn on your lights. If you want to go boating, honk your horn." The noise would be deafening.

Our lives are comprised completely of have-tos and want-tos. We enjoy the things we want to do; the things we have to do, we are usually not too excited about. Why is it that so many Americans do not enjoy their jobs? Because in their work, their choices are usually severely limited. They are told exactly what to do and *how* to do it. They don't have very much fun. And they don't perform as well as they do when they are having fun.

In *A Passion for Excellence*, Tom Peters and Nancy Austin

describe the freedom of choice at W. L. Gore and Associates, Inc. When new employees come on board, they aren't *given* an assignment. They are allowed to wander around for a few weeks and *find* an assignment. "We organize ourselves around voluntary commitments," says Gore. I once had an opportunity to meet one of Gore's associates while on a business trip. I asked her if they really operate in that fashion. She said, "That's exactly the way we run it."

In recreation, people can choose to do what they excel at. As a result, they succeed. If they want to play golf, they can play golf. If they want to play tennis, they can play tennis. How many times have you heard someone say, "Well, I have to go skiing today"? I'm a downhill skier—by choice. But cross-country skiers don't think I get any exercise, and snowboarders look at a mountain slope in a totally different way.

The greatest skiers in the world may not make very good golfers, but nobody is forcing them to play golf. The same principle holds true in business; the more choices you give your employees— within the bounds of your business, of course—the better they will perform, and the more they will enjoy it.

If you give your players more freedom, a few may decide to do just enough to get by. Of course, that's probably all they are doing with the freedom they have now. But many of your players will do more and achieve more than you ever dreamed possible. Why? Because most people become committed to what they freely choose. People need to own their jobs, and they can own them only if they have a choice about what their jobs are, about what their goals are, and about how they will reach those goals.

Winners don't seek to change the rules; they only seek to understand them well enough to win. So is it with choice. You must recognize which choices are yours to make and which ones you can't worry about.

I now realize that in my athletic career if I could have changed the stickiness of a football at the moment it was being thrown to me in a crowded stadium, I would have been all-pro, without a doubt. There were times in a stadium when I was open, that the quarterback delivered that football right into my hands, and I could have caught it if the thing had been just a little stickier. I had no choice about that, but I did have a choice on how to cut on that defensive back. I had choices on my technique, whether to punt cross-handed or with an over-hand grip. I had choices in my methods.

And in the workplace, if you will trust your people to make the choices that they can make, they will become winners. There are leaders that treat people as if they were important or unimportant. To people they consider important, they insist on explaining why, to unimportant people, they simply tell how. We can tell how someone feels about us by the way they talk to us. Important people are allowed to make choices. Unimportant people have their choices restricted. What you need to look at is what you are communicating about your players based on the choices you allow them to make.

Workers need to understand the reasons behind the things you ask them to do. They need to help negotiate the results that are expected. They need to be allowed to help determine what the company will become, because when they go home and talk to their neighbors, they are their company, and they need to have a choice about what they are. Finally, after all these things have been settled, people need to be allowed to use whatever methods they are comfortable with to bring the goals to pass.

If people had always insisted on doing things the way their predecessors did, we would have none of the progress we have had; but progress has come from those people who were willing to think outside the usual limits, even with their eyes clearly on the goal, and who have figured out better, different, and faster ways to do things.

DECISION MAKING

People who can make good decisions are some of the most sought-after people in American business. We celebrate decision makers. We want to have them in our companies. But if we're not willing to advance the challenge of choice to beginning players, from the day they come in the door, about where their desks sit, about how their offices are decorated, about all of the things that give them a sense of ownership and don't detract at all from the long-term success of the company, we can't build the decision makers of tomorrow.

Are you encouraging choice? Are you asking for innovation? Do you make clear what things in your company can't be changed and in what things workers are free to choose?

BEHAVIOR

Our choices are our behavior, and we cannot change the result without changing the behavior. That's a frightening lesson for many of us to learn, but a true one. I cannot get consequence B by behaving in way A. "I would like to lose weight as long as I don't have to give up the hot fudge." "I want to be financially independent but I can't give up my credit cards." "I'd like to be a marathon runner, but don't ask me to run in the rain." "I'd like to compete in downhill skiing, but I don't want to take lessons."

There's no way to get around the fact that behavior precedes results. As the behavior of players determines the team results, so does the behavior of workers and managers determine the success of a business. Too often businesses try to blame outside influences if they don't get desired results, when it's the way the players behave that determines whether or not the team wins with any degree of consistency.

We can go one step further: Attitude is the prime cause of behavior.

ATTITUDE

The way I *think* determines the way I will *act*, whether it is in a momentary fit of rage or in contemplation in a planning session. It is imperative to understand that the thought precedes the act. Also, it is impossible to behave *consistently* contrary to a basic attitude. We may behave contrary to our values at times, by coercion or inducement, but not consistently.

This brings us to a problem facing most coaches. They may be able to specify what behavior is required in a player to produce the desired result, but they don't know how to mold the attitude so the desired behavior can be achieved.

There are two powerful forces that form attitudes. One is a significant emotional event. The death of a loved one while participating in a sport may significantly shape our attitude toward that sport. A severe reprimand from the first boss may shape a worker's attitude toward management for years to come. Significant emotional events, while necessary and recognized attitude modifiers, are not easily duplicated in coaching environments. They are difficult to control.

The second formative force in attitude is conditioning. Conditioning is the same force that trains the dog with the electric collar or makes Pavlov's dogs salivate when the bell is rung.

CONDITIONING

You don't have an electric collar, but you must admit that your past conditioning influences the way you act. You may have been reared with these statements:

"Children should be seen and not heard."
"Never bite off more than you can chew."
"Never speak unless spoken to."

"Never go where you're not wanted."

"Never talk to strangers."

If you're in a marketing role, your entire job description is contrary to the great parental advice that kept you safely out of the clutches of kidnappers on your way to school. The cornerstone of sales-call reluctance in the American sales force was planted there on those sidewalks to kindergarten.

If you don't believe me, walk into the nearest elevator and recognize that it's a six-by-eight-foot American institution where fourteen strangers can stand close enough to touch each other and nobody talks. We all duck in, turn around, and look at the numbers above the door.

The next time you get into an elevator, do not turn around. Simply face your fellow passengers. Watch their eyes go to the floor. And if you feel bold, say, "Good morning, how are you?" Conditioning does shape attitudes.

What makes conditioning such a powerful force? Repetition, repetition, repetition. We did not learn to avoid strangers because we were told once, but because most of us were told every time we left the house to be wary of strangers. Perhaps all of our parents went to school together and learned to say the same things to their children. None of us was brash enough to turn around as we left the house and wonder what our other choices were. It didn't occur to us to question the source of that information. But today, how many of our investment philosophies or management decisions are guided by those youthful admonitions?

Today, how many of us "look before we leap," "save our money for a rainy day," and "make sure that if we can't say something nice about somebody we don't say anything at all"? This last one has had a great impact on restricting management discipline.

REPETITION

When you are coaching you must understand that success is the result of behavior, which is determined by attitudes, which are formed by conditioning, which takes place through repetition.

Repetitive learning is the only vehicle to modify conditioning, which alters the attitudes that control our behavior, which produces the results we want. One trip, one lecture, one seminar, one tape won't do it. Advertisers say it takes eight repetitions before the consumer will even notice your product.

Winners understand the importance of conditioning as it relates to attitudes, behavior, and eventually achieving success or results. Winners are constantly conditioning themselves by reviewing their written goals, reading good books, surrounding themselves with other goal-oriented individuals, and inviting repetition of positive thoughts while pushing negative thoughts out of their minds.

You can bet the Indianapolis Colts don't make up very many plays during the course of a game. The bread-and-butter plays of their offense have been rehearsed in practice dozens, if not hundreds, of times. The players are conditioned by repetition to respond in a predetermined way to each play number.

Winners in business also understand the conditioning process and the need for repetition, and they do everything in their power to use this powerful force to achieve success and results.

Repetition influences our conditioning. Our conditioning influences our attitudes. And our attitudes influence our behavior— the things we choose to do. Thus, we can directly influence ourselves and our people to make the choices that will bring success.

I once consulted with a company that built modular housing. The carpenters worked inside a factory. We had been tracking the total square footage produced by the workers, and it totaled about 44,000 square feet of finished housing in five days. It was the week of the deer hunt, and some of the supervisors went to the vice president of manufacturing and said, "We would like to get off work early Friday." The vice president said, "If you get 44,000 square feet done by Friday at noon, you can leave then." I suggested that we should see what would happen if we allowed the workers to choose the day they could get off work as long as the 44,000 feet of work was finished. The vice president took my suggestion, and the workers did leave work early—at 2:00 on Wednesday. The plumbers and the electricians and the roofers all helped each other, and the work was done in record time. Why? Because they had a choice. Before that they had to work until Friday at 5:00. They *had* to. But when they had the opportunity to do what they *wanted* to do, they were willing to do it.

If you want to motivate your workers, if you want them to feel like members of the team, if you want them to work as if the company belonged to them, you must give them the freedom to choose the way to succeed. If you do, they will come through for you—beyond your wildest dreams.

·SIX·

Field of Play

Great managers constantly seek to minimize uncertainty.
CHUCK COONRADT

Who could forget Rosie Ruiz in the 1980 Boston Marathon? She finished first among the female contestants. Her time, compared to her past performances, was unbelievably good. Why? Because outside the field of play, outside the rules of competition, she made it to the finish line without having run the race which, of course, greatly improved her time. She had finished the race, but her performance was not within the criteria established by those who controlled the race. Her time was not recorded in the record book, and there is no Boston Marathon walk-from-the-hotel trophy. The Boston Marathon has a clearly defined field of play, and Rosie got herself into trouble by trying to perform outside the field of play.

In organizations of every kind, we hear the cry to improve communication. Improving communication is the topic of millions of conversations every day. This problem isn't nearly as serious on the playing field among athletes as it is in business. How many of the sixty or so plays in a football game are not communicated to the players? Very few, if any.

People keep trying to solve communication problems. We've seen the era of transactional analysis. We've gone through sensitivity training and empathy building and role playing. We've had the job description writers, and I must admit an incredible bias against their efforts—mainly because of their lack of specificity and the necessity of the Supreme Court to interpret the language of many job descriptions. A client of mine, a president of a company generating net profits in the millions, had a fourteen-page job description, and the only numbers contained therein were the page numbers. It's very difficult to understand success and failure, winning and losing, good and bad, in that morass of confusion.

Before we develop our goals, we must establish certain criteria about our field of play. When Dr. James Naismith hung that first peach basket up on the barn wall and started the game of basketball, he had to define the dimensions of the field of play. He had to set the rules. He had to identify to the players when their baskets would count and when they would not, where they could dribble and where they would be out-of-bounds. And when Abner Doubleday organized the sport of baseball, the primary improvement he brought to the previous activities of throwing rocks at squirrels and hitting chestnuts with sticks was the design and dimension of the field of play.

If you were given several acres of raw ground and given the assignment to lay it out for a sports center, one of your design techniques might be to take scale models of the various fields of play and begin arranging them on that property in order to make the best use of space. It would make no sense to stick a basketball standard here, a hockey goal there, and a baseball backstop over here without knowing implications of the decision.

You can't go out and start playing until your field of play is clearly and completely established. The boundaries must be in place before you can set the goals and begin to play the game. Even in a casual game of touch football or sandlot baseball, the kids will decide the boundaries before they start playing.

In sports, fields of play are so well known they are almost taken for granted. If I say, "Let's go play tennis," you correctly assume that we're going to a tennis court. If I say, "Grab your golf clubs," your only question is which course we are going to play on.

The shape of the field says so much about the nature of the game that it is incredible to me that we have not done a better job in business in defining the field of play before we just run off with an SUV loaded with equipment or drop a new computer on a manager's desk.

Our problem, I think, lies in the fact that in recreation the fields of play exist already. They've always just been there. So we walk onto them and accept the assumptions they give us without really thinking about them. We've never had to create fields of play, and we have not been taught how to do it.

What shape is the field of play in basketball? A rectangle. What is a tennis court? Again a rectangle. A football field is a rectangle, too. What shape is a racetrack? Oval. A baseball diamond is not a diamond, but actually a square, and if you look at the entire field you find a quarter of a circle. We couldn't play any of these games without first accepting the standard field of play. What do you think would be the reaction at the New York City Athletic Club if an unknown college running back walked in the door and announced that he had come for the Heisman Trophy?

"But I rushed over three thousand yards this year!" claims the player as he is led to the exit.

"We don't have any record of that."

"Ask the coach. He saw me. I did it during practice."

"But that doesn't count."

The point here is that if you are going to play a game, you've got to know where the out-of-bounds markers are. You must have a general overview of the field of competition. You can't take credit for performance outside your assigned area.

You may be wondering why I even bother to discuss such an obvious principle. I do so because you can find hundreds of business examples—common, everyday occurrences—where people are expected to perform without knowing the field of play. Our ability to overlook the obvious is incredible.

FIELDS OF PLAY IN BUSINESS

Consider the employee who has just come out of a retail staff meeting where he has been chewed out for allowing excessive customer returns.

"We took back a thirty-five-dollar DVD player yesterday that was purchased almost a year ago," scolded the manager. "How can we expect to make money when employees are that ignorant of company policy?"

Two hours later the employee is waiting unknowingly on a good friend of the manager who wants to return something that wasn't purchased in the store. The manager knows she is a very good customer. The employee knows what he heard in the morning meeting. The manager and the employee have different perceptions of the field of play, which has never been clearly defined.

As the employee courteously explains to the customer why the company cannot accept the returned merchandise, the manager walks up and says, "Good morning, Mrs. Fishburg. How are you? Glad to have you in our store today. Of course we'll take your return."

The employee is suddenly confused. The field of play is no longer clear, and for the rest of the day that employee would just as soon hide in a corner. You cannot change the rules in the middle of the game without destroying the self-confidence of the player.

Can you remember a situation in your business where someone overstepped their bounds, played outside their sandbox, and messed up someone else's job because they didn't have a clear understanding of their field of play? You can probably think of lots of examples.

Can you think of anyone in business with a clearly defined field of play? Someone who works in an environment of absolute certainty with clear policies and procedures—clear work rules, security, guarantees, a certain amount of vacation—a person who knows exactly what to do every day? You might have in mind someone who works on an assembly line or perhaps runs a mail-sorting machine at the post office. You may think people with such jobs are not happy because they are not challenged. They don't have the variety, fun, and risk that you might have, but they do have a high comfort level, a very high degree of certainty.

In such cases, people have a field of play that is similar to a square. A square is symmetrical, and the sides are a certain length. Nobody has any question about what its boundaries are. In business, freedom is greatest when boundaries are clearly defined. When I know exactly where the edge is, I am more confident. I would rather be following a police officer in his car than be concerned about him hiding in an alleyway with his radar gun. I would rather drive on a treacherous patch of icy road when I have clear vision than I would when I'm in the fog. My freedom and security are greatest when my boundaries are clearly defined.

I was driving with a broken speedometer cable to a city thirty miles north of my home one day. I was late for an appointment, and I'd received two speeding tickets in the previous ninety days; one more and they would take away my driver's license. The uncertainty was incredible.

I'd look at my watch and be reminded that I was running late. I would speed up. Then, realizing I was passing other cars, I figured I was going too fast and would slow down. Every time I came over a hill, I fully expected to see a highway patrol car with a radar gun waiting for me. Gradually the uncertainty forced me to restrict my performance, to shrink back. Since I didn't know where the boundaries were, I had to restrict my performance in an effort to avoid going out-of-bounds. With two speeding tickets already, I simply couldn't take that risk. Had my speedometer been working, I could have moved comfortably to the very edge of the boundary at sixty miles an hour without any anxiety, knowing I was within the field of play.

Sometimes we find ourselves in a field of play shaped like a doughnut. We have a large area of responsibility and a small area of authority. This is the frustration of many people in administrative roles or staff positions who are given broad parameters of what line management expects but little authority to carry out those expectations. Their response is to wander about the company saying, "Charles told me . . . ," "Charles says . . . ," "Charles wants us to . . . ," and they are never really sure about the authority they represent and can find no satisfaction in their own authority. The doughnut, unfortunately, becomes a center where very little is accomplished, where people "dough-not" do anything.

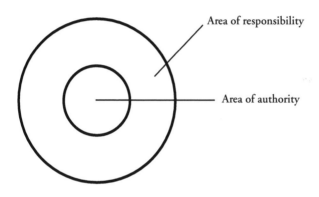

In the early days of home computers there was a mad rush into the field, with dozens of companies competing vigorously for market share. Rebates and price cutting were common fare as manufacturers pushed their wares on confused retailers. The result was an oversupply of home computers, resulting in downward price pressure. Most of these aggressive computer manufacturers not only found themselves without profit but in a struggle for survival. No one bothered to set the boundaries before they started to play the game. Market sizes, demographics, buying patterns, and customer profiles were not clearly defined. Without a clear field of play, the result was chaos.

Another common field of play in business is shaped like an amoeba—a random, globular shape. It describes the employee's understanding of what he or she thinks is expected, and the only problem is that it wiggles and jiggles and changes shape. When something goes wrong that the employee didn't think was his or her responsibility, sure enough, someone points it out as his or her responsibility on the amoeba.

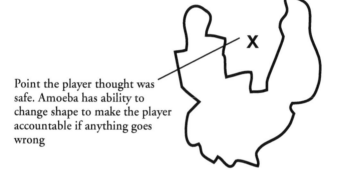

Point the player thought was safe. Amoeba has ability to change shape to make the player accountable if anything goes wrong

As mentioned earlier, the ideal field of play may be represented by a square. The only real problem with the square is that it has a limit. If we were to take one side off the square and provide a growth outlet, then I believe we would have an ideal field of play for business, as in the following diagram.

On the left side of the field of play are the terminal out-of-bounds—those things that, if players did them, they would immediately be fired, such as embezzling company funds. On the right side are the operational out-of-bounds—things that players are not allowed to do while working, such as wearing a T-shirt and jeans to a sales presentation. They would not be fired, but they might be sent home to change. At the bottom of the field is the performance out-of-bounds—the area where the employees are simply not performing.

Paydirt

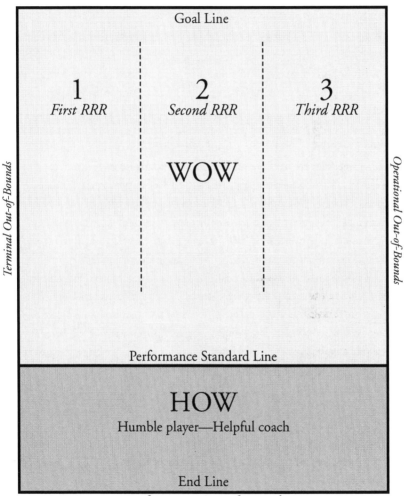

The players may not be removed from the team, but they may be transferred to a new area of responsibility.

The HOW is really the first word in the coaching statement "How can I help?" Meaning that the coach is ready to give his or her full attention and experience to helping the player select a course of action that will return their performance to above the performance standard. In this area, the players are expected to be humble, to accept the guidance of the coach. And the coach is expected to be helpful, to do what he or she can to get the player to meet the minimum standard.

WOW means exactly that. The coach is the cheerleader. Giving positive reinforcement for results above the performance standard. Players with results in this area are given great freedom. This is the area where the players are performing above the minimum accepted standard. Here, they are given great freedom to play the game however they wish within the rules to achieve the goals they have set. They are not subject to close scrutiny or oversupervision, although they may use the coach as a resource as needed.

The areas marked 1, 2, and 3 are the three results-to-resources ratios for which the players are responsible. Your employees may have only one, or they may have more. This is up to you and them.

Across the goal line is the pay dirt, where the players receive those special levels of compensation or privileges that are reserved for those who turn in exceptional performances.

You should sit down with every one of your employees and with every new employee that joins your team and define with them these elements on their field of play, especially as the field of play may differ for every employee.

The first thing you should define is what constitutes terminal and operational out-of-bounds.

One time I was working with a fast-food company that had

seven outlets. In the middle of a discussion of fear and expectations, I turned to one of the managers and said, "Dave, do you have any fear in this company?"

He said, "Oh, I've got a bunch of it."

"What are you afraid of?" I asked.

"I'm afraid of being fired."

It got rather hushed in the room because the owner-president was there with the supervisory staff and administrative people. I was prompted to ask, "Dave, since you're afraid of being fired, tell me one thing that you know if you were doing it, you'd be gone."

He thought for a moment and then said, "I don't know."

Think about it. *A person in almost constant fear who did not know what would get him fired.*

It seemed like a good idea to persist in the questioning. I asked the same question of the next manager and received the same response. All the managers had the same fear. I take my hat off to the president and owner of that company, who sat silently, taking a rather bitter pill. As I met with him later in an individual conference, he relayed his astonishment that he had not been more aware of his managers' fear of losing their jobs. I assured him that his situation was not unusual and suggested that we correct it by listing the things he felt were serious enough to justify terminating a relationship.

At the next meeting with the managers, the eighteen-point list was passed around. The room was silent as the managers read the list with great interest. Then, one by one, sighs began to come forth from each of the participants, and Dave, our first manager, summed it up the best when he said, "But I'm not doing any of these things."

To which the president responded, "Then, Dave, you have nothing to worry about."

At The Game of Work, we establish what constitutes the terminal and operational out-of-bounds in our company with an

"Out-of-Bounds Statement." In this statement, we spell out exactly what will cause a player to be fired, and we make no apologies about it. If employees don't like these conditions, they are free to seek employment elsewhere. And if they agree to these conditions, they are free from worry about what might cause them to lose their job. They already *know* what might cause them to lose it, so they can then concentrate on winning within the rules and without fear.

After you have explained to the players what constitutes out-of-bounds, you must define with them the other areas on the field of play. At The Game of Work, we do this in writing with our "Field of Play Development Agenda" and our "Field of Play Coaching Meetings Agenda." By reading through these agendas and their supporting documents (which are also reproduced here), you will be able to get a good idea of how we define the fields of play in our organization. Then you may want to take a similar course in yours, using our documents as models. We bind the documents together with a cover page, and we call this collection of documents our "Field of Play Agreement." It allows us to make clear to our workers exactly what is expected of them.

How you define the field of play to your players is not really important. But what is important is that you *do* define it accurately and clearly in a way that works for your organization.

FIELD OF PLAY

OUT-OF-BOUNDS STATEMENT

Terminal Out-of-Bounds

Because our business is built on trust and respect for our integrity and professionalism, we must be above reproach. Therefore, those things that will result in being subject to immediate termination of employment if engaged in are:

1. Embezzlement or theft; any misappropriation of money due; misappropriations of supplies, inventories, or trade secrets.

2. Any violation of copyrights held by the company, its principals, or any other supplier of material that may result in endangering our agreements.

3. Failure to perform a service for which we have been contracted or been paid.

4. Using company, representation, or the contacts you have made as a result of your employment or developed expertise to perform any service like or similar to our services which is not billed through the company.

5. Lying or any misrepresentation of the facts concerning status of a sale, an account receivable, or the whereabouts or behavior of self or a fellow employee.

6. Any adultery or fornication or immoral relationship with another employee, or an employee of any client companies.

7. Disorderly behavior that is alcohol or drug induced in the presence of a client, whether you are working or socializing, or are observed by the client.

8. Any declaration to another individual(s) that is disloyal, degrading, or defamatory of the company, its officers, or its employees.

9. Failure to treat any employee, client employee, or client as an individual.

10. Any behavior, public or private, that detracts from the ethical and professional reputation of the company.

Operational Out-of-Bounds

1. Failure to attend two consecutive regularly scheduled meetings without approval.

Signed: _____ Date: _____

FIELD OF PLAY

DEVELOPMENT AGENDA

Recommendations

1. Compile a Field of Play folder for each agreement (one copy each to coach and player). The folder contains:

   A. Field of Play diagram [see p. 79]

   B. Out-of-bounds statements—terminal and operational [see p. 83]

   C. Expectancy statements from player and coach [see p. 91]

   D. Three to five scorecards on areas of measurable performance

2. Each team member negotiates his/her agreement as a player before initiating any agreements as a coach.

First Meeting

Date Completed

_____ 1. Coach establishes written Out-of-Bounds

   A. Terminal

   1. Company-wide

   2. Individual applications

   B. Operational

_____ 2. Coach suggests three to five areas for scorekeeping (sales per day, average order, gross profit per transaction).

_____ 3. Coach completes an expectation statement for the player (will include all responsibilities not scorecarded as stated above).

Second Meeting (To be held within seven days of first meeting.)

Date Completed

_____   1. Player suggests additional areas for scorekeeping.

_____   2. Player provides his expectancy statement.

Third Meeting (To be completed within seven days of second meeting.)

Date Completed

_____   1. Player suggests minimum performance standards for these areas of measurement.

_____   2. Player suggests pay-dirt levels and desired rewards.

_____   3. Negotiation and agreement on all performance areas.

_____   4. Agree on frequency of reporting.

_____   5. Ask what help is needed and what resources are needed.

Instructions for Using the One-on-One Coaching Diagram
(Field of Play—Coaching Meeting Agenda – Meeting 4 and Ongoing)

1. Consistency is critical. We recommend you conduct coaching meetings at least monthly, if at all possible. Many coaches and players find it's easier to develop the habit of conducting regular meetings by scheduling it on the same day and time each month, e.g. the first Monday, the last Friday, the third Tuesday, etc.

2. The atmosphere of the meeting needs to be comfortable, nonthreatening, and free of interruptions, except emergencies.

3. Use the Diagram for One-on-One Coaching as an agenda and track to run on.

4. When conducted regularly, the meetings don't need to be longer than one or two hours.

5. Use the first half of the time allotted to review the process of your business. It is best to review the coach's and player's scorecards in priority order.

    a. Give appropriate feedback

        i. Celebrate successes when in the WOW zone

        ii. Offer help and/or develop "plays" when in the HOW zone

6. One-third of the remaining time is devoted to discussing goals in priority order.

    a. What has been accomplished since the last coaching meeting?

    b. What will be accomplished by the next coaching meeting?

7. One-third of the remaining time is devoted to discussing projects in priority order. Projects might be obstacles that need to be removed to accomplish a goal, new opportunities that need to be developed, or routine things that "pop up" in the process of doing business.

    a. What has been accomplished since the last coaching meeting?

    b. What will be accomplished by the next coaching meeting?

8. The remaining one-third of the time is devoted to people development—both coach and player.

    a. What behaviors do player and coach need to start doing?

    b. What behaviors do player and coach need to stop doing?

    c. What behaviors do player and coach need to accelerate?

9. Conclude the coaching session by recapping the action steps (or have the player recap) and affirm the player's worth and value to the organization.

DIAGRAM FOR

ONE-ON-ONE COACHING

(Field of Play — Meeting 4 and Ongoing)

PLAYER:_____ COACH:_____ DATE:_____

I. PROCESS OF OUR BUSINESS

Scorecard Review
Discuss in Descending Order
Give Appropriate Feedback

WOW   HOW

CELEBRATE   PLAYS (Post-it Notes)

II. GOALS—PLANNING SHEET
New Sheet Created Quarterly

Last Thirty-Day Steps Completed
1. _____
2. _____
3. _____
4. _____

Next Thirty-Day Steps Completed
1. _____
2. _____
3. _____
4. _____

III. PROJECTS
New Sheet Created Quarterly

Last Thirty-Day Steps Completed
1. _____
2. _____
3. _____
4. _____

Next Thirty-Day Steps Completed
1. _____
2. _____
3. _____
4. _____

IV. PLAYER DEVELOPMENT
WHAT WILL WE

Keep _____

Accelerate _____

Start _____

Stop _____

TOGETHER!
"Prioritization is the saving grace of a busy life."

FIELD OF PLAY

COACH'S EXPECTATIONS

1. Have a career orientation.

2. Be a conscientious counselor.

3. Support the performer.

4. Give 110 percent support, especially in front of members of The Game of Work team.

5. Be positive and specific.

6. Negatives come up to the coach. Positives go down to the players.

7. Write all unresolved questions at least weekly and send to me.

8. Expect growth through new tasks and assignments and techniques. Admit self-imposed limitations and attack past negative conditioning.

9. Be a product of the product. Personal goals and scorekeeping program current, up-to-date, and worthy to be demonstrated.

10. Expect and use "why" communication—if not provided, ask.

11. Trust coach's motives to have your best interests at heart.

A clearly outlined field of play results in certainty and consistency. And only after the field of play is established can realistic goals be set. You need to know where the field is before you can set the goals. In recreation we start with a clear definition of the boundaries, and we establish goals within those boundaries. In business, many times we start by establishing goals without first having the boundaries clearly in place. That's why it's often difficult to know if goals are realistic or not. The boundaries must precede the placement of goals in business as well as in sports.

To be an effective coach obviously requires more than creating a playbook and a file cabinet full of field of play agreements. You must dedicate time to coaching.

The most effective way to do this is with a one-on-one uninterrupted coaching session with *each* player every month. *Every month.* If you are employing someone on a forty-hour week, or 173 hours a month, it isn't too much to ask that less than 1 percent of his time be earmarked for specific direction.

I know we give orders and instructions. We have staff meetings and team meetings and meetings to plan meetings. But I am talking here about coaching sessions, one-on-one, bare-knuckles, quality time taken with each individual player.

No coach would want to enter a critical game, part of a championship series, and have someone say, "Sorry, coach, you can't have any time-outs, no halftime with the players, no time between quarters." No coach would accept that, yet in business we seem perfectly willing to accept job descriptions with annual or semiannual review sessions.

Managers at The Game of Work and at the client companies who have adopted The Game of Work philosophy make sure that people are coached frequently and regularly. They do this with the cover page of the Field of Play Agreement, which is a schedule agreed upon by player and coach as to the specific dates and times coaching sessions will take place. The Field of Play Agreement is the most important document available in American business today. Why? Because it ensures that coaching and feedback will take place. It can be updated each month, or more often if performance (or lack thereof) warrants it. It is simple. It is straightforward. It is specific. Most of all, it is effective. The cover page of our Field of Play Agreement looks like the following page.

Feedback can never become too frequent, as long as it is honest and positive. Create a schedule so that your players know in advance when their hour arrives. If your span of control is too large for you to give this kind of quality coaching, spin off some of your people and build a second level of management. Get some assistant coaches. But do not hang onto a system that does not allow feedback from your people.

One of the biggest problems in business today is people are not being told what is expected of them. Every person has the right to personal freedoms and self-determination, but to get the job done—in sports as well as in business—somebody has to stand up and say, "This is what we are going to do, and this is how we are going to do it."

In the absence of a clearly defined field of play, uncertainty thrives and performance suffers. With a clearly defined field of play, players know the boundaries within which it is possible to win.

FIELD OF PLAY AGREEMENT

Between

COACH:_____ DATE: _____

PLAYER: _____ POSITION: _____

1ˢᵗ Meeting

DATE:_____ COACH: _____PLAYER: _____

2ⁿᵈ Meeting

DATE:_____ COACH: _____PLAYER: _____

3ʳᵈ Meeting

DATE:_____ COACH: _____PLAYER: _____

1st Monthly Meeting

DATE:_____ COACH: _____PLAYER: _____

·seven·

Winning

Everybody is born with an equal chance to become just as unequal as he or she possibly can.

ANONYMOUS

Can you list the names of the five teams Pittsburgh has beaten in the Super Bowl? While you're working on that one, give me the names of the cyclists who finished as runners-up to Lance Armstrong in his seven Tour de France victories. And then after you get that, give me the golfers who finished second to Tiger Woods when he won his Masters' green jackets.

If you're having a tough time answering these questions, then you realize that the answer is the same: Who cares? Only winners are remembered. Don't let anybody tell you that winning isn't important.

There's a company in Salt Lake City that manufactures NFL insignia merchandise—part of a billion-dollar industry. The biggest customers are twenty-five- to twenty-nine-year-old fathers who didn't make it in football and are now hoping that through insignia osmosis their kids will do better.

Hundreds of companies throughout the country manufacture NFL merchandise. Almost half of all NFL merchandise sold each year bears the logos of the Division Championship game participants. Why? Because everybody likes to do business with a winner.

Why do we use Olympic gold medalists and Super Bowl champions for all those shoe and drink commercials? Why don't we pick amateur athletes or semi-pro ball players? Wouldn't it be a lot cheaper? You know the answer. We pick the familiar because of the recognition value and the fact that everybody likes to do business with a winner.

Look at it this way. If you accidentally kill somebody with your car, who would you want to represent you in court? The top criminal attorney in the country with over a hundred court wins under his belt, or some kid still in law school who thinks he or she can do a pretty good job but has never won a case in court? You would want to go with the winner, of course.

One of the premier high priests of winning in America was Vince Lombardi, former head coach of the Green Bay Packers. He said, "Winning isn't everything, it's the only thing."

The coach was criticized for that statement. Some said he placed too much emphasis on winning, that he should have put more emphasis on sportsmanship. Some of Lombardi's critics put together a new kind of baseball league for kids in a Texas community. It was like the Little League—the same ball, same bat, same number of innings, same playing field—everything was the same except that they didn't keep score. The idea was that there wouldn't be any losers because nobody would know who won.

Do you know how long it lasted? One and a half innings. The kids walked across the street to play sandlot ball where they could keep score. Winning is important!

There's a lot being said today in America about fairness. Everything is supposed to be fair, and there are a lot of people who think that fair and equal are the same thing. Winners have a different philosophy that can be summed up in the following: "Everybody's born with the equal chance to become just as unequal as he or she possibly can."

A second thing Coach Lombardi said was, "The objective is to win fairly, squarely, by the rules, but to win." One of his great tackles, a guy by the name of Henry Jordan, had become a phenomenal salesman. Henry was asked one time, "Henry, why do you like to sell?" He said, "Because of the competition." He explained that every time a salesman meets a potential customer, a sale is made. Either the customer buys the product, or the salesman buys the customer's excuse.

A third thing Lombardi said is, "You don't win once in a while. You don't win occasionally. You don't win by accident. Winning is a habit, just like losing."

The following are seven characteristics of winners.

WINNERS ARE PREPARED

Winners are ready to play. They don't show up for sales appointments without order forms. They don't show up without a game plan.

George Allen coached the Washington Redskins and took them to Super Bowl VII in 1973. Allen paid a guy for a week to sit on the thirty-yard line in the Los Angeles Coliseum so he'd know what the angle of the sun would be during the entire ball game. Allen wanted to know which goal to defend when the coin was tossed. Winners are prepared.

How long does it take to reach the Super Bowl? The correct technical answer is twenty-four hours. That's right, twenty-four sixty-minute games—four preseason contests, sixteen regular season games, and four playoff contests. Were twenty-four hours of preparation involved in preparing for each of those sixty-minute games? When you consider the time of the coaches, players, trainers—on and off the field—you wouldn't have any trouble counting up thousands of hours of preparation for each of those sixty-minute games.

In business, too often our dedication to constant activity eliminates the essential focus on preparation. If we are to be or to produce winners in our companies, we must take the time to prepare. We must take time to clearly define our results-to-resources ratios for each of our key performers. We must take the time to give them the opportunity to construct a game plan, scout the competition, and build a strategy before we simply send them out to play.

WINNERS EXPECT TO WIN

Tiger Woods won three U.S. Amateur championships before turning pro. Did he expect to win? You bet. In fact, the power of expectation was so strong, the man he beat in his third championship said, "I knew when I was only five holes up with nine to play that I didn't have a big enough lead." Tiger Woods saw himself as a winner and made a bigger splash in the Amateur golf circuit than any in recent memory or maybe even of all time. That behavior continued on in his first major tournament victory. Less than three months later he defeated an established veteran in sudden death. "I always expect to win, and I always expect the shot to go where I intend it go." It may be difficult to differentiate this self-assurance from unfounded cockiness, but the proof is in the performance. And the winners always expect to win. Always.

Two and a half decades before, Broadway Joe Namath—upstart, young, and cocky—predicted that the New York Jets would win Super Bowl III. In the first two Super Bowls, the AFL champion had been beaten easily by the Green Bay Packers. And nobody expected the Baltimore Colts to stumble. But Joe Namath expected to win, and he delivered.

WINNERS ARE SPECIFIC AND POSITIVE

Losers tend to be general and negative. Negativism is the antithesis of a winning attitude. Negativism is the most destructive force that any of us come in contact with, because it robs us of those good feelings we should have about ourselves. Negativism is an evil force. Negativism is like a cancer of the mind.

I once had a young man working for me who was assigned the task of setting up sales calls, making appointments. He called in about 4:30 one afternoon, and I said, "How's it going, Richard?"

He said, "How do you get past these secretaries?"

"I don't understand," I said.

"None of them will let me see their bosses," he explained.

Anytime I hear a negative generalization I immediately want to dig into it. I said, "Tell me how the day went."

"I made twenty calls," he said. "Fourteen of the bosses weren't even in."

I knew right off that 70 percent of the secretaries did not refuse to let him talk to their bosses. Their bosses weren't in.

"Tell me about the other six," I said.

"I got two appointments, and two people are going to call me back."

"The other two?"

"One had to leave in the middle of the conversation, and the other, well, her secretary . . ."

See what this salesman did? One of twenty calls went sour, so he made a negative generalization about the whole day's work. When you describe a negative situation, always be ultra-specific. Don't let the negative wandering generality rob you of a positive mental attitude.

Winners see their drinking glasses as half full, not half empty. Winners see the opportunity, losers see the problems. We have heard those comments before. If you have employees who are constantly looking at the empty half of the glass, you may want to focus on changing their performance *and* correcting their negative attitude.

WINNERS ACCEPT PERSONAL RESPONSIBILITY FOR THEIR ACTIONS

Winners say "I," "me," and "our." Losers say "they," "them," "those guys," and "management." Losers use the language of noncommitment.

I was meeting with the manager of a company one time, and I asked, "Do you have any problems in this company?"

"Yes," he said, "we have two."

This is going to be easy, I thought. This guy has his problems all netted out.

"What is the first one?" I asked.

"Management doesn't care." As he spoke he extended his right arm straight to the ceiling and locked his elbow.

"What's the second one?" I asked.

"The employees don't care either." He extended his left arm toward the floor and again locked his elbow.

"May I ask you a question?" I asked.

He nodded.

"Which group do you fit into?"

He looked stunned. Finally, he said, "You know, I never

thought of it like that before."

He had an acute case of loser's elbow. It's like tennis elbow, that ailment tennis players get when they serve too hard or don't hit the ball dead center.

Loser's elbow is most common in management and sales meetings. For instance, when the boss asks why the report isn't finished, somebody says, "Peggy didn't get it done." *Pop* goes the elbow. The boss asks why she didn't get it done. Somebody says, "The IT department didn't get the network up." *Pop*, there it goes again. The IT department gets blamed for most of the late reports in the world.

Another word popular with losers is *economy*. When the boss asks how sales were last month, the elbow goes pop when someone responds, "Well, you know how the economy is."

Inflation is another big word in the vocabularies of losers. Inflation is the sum total of all the increases in prices. Generally it affects your revenues as well as your expenses, the net difference being zero. That's all. Yet the decision-making politicians at the head of our government would like us to believe that inflation is the cause of our economic woes. They've got pains in their elbows, too.

Just as important in the language of noncommitment is *computer*. Ever hear of a shipment that didn't get out because of a computer? As if the computer is responsible for pulling the order, walking into the warehouse, and throwing a box on a truck. If computers were really responsible for half of what they get blamed for, companies would quit buying them.

Then there is the language of noncommitment related to places. Ever hear a receptionist say with the greatest tone of importance, "San Francisco's on the phone."

That would be something, a conference call with eight hundred thousand people, all at once.

Or the guy who asks about the pay raise he was promised and

is told that Chicago turned him down. And he didn't even know he was on the ballot.

The problem with loser's elbow is that your arm eventually locks into the losing position, making it tough for you to get through doorways when they open up. Somebody will say, "Hey, you did a super job on that project." And you will respond, "Well, not really, but wait until tomorrow." Winners accept personal responsibility, whether they are winning or losing.

The story of Julio and Jenny illustrates the acceptance of responsibility through the language of commitment.

It seems that Julio and Jenny were going to market early one morning and met at the crossroads.

"Good morning," said Julio.

"I'm not supposed to be talking to you," responded Jenny.

"And why not?" asked Julio, hurt by her blunt reply.

"Julio," she explained, "we are all alone here. There is no one else around. If I were to be friendly to you, you might attempt to steal a kiss."

"Jenny, how could I possibly do that?" he asked with a shocked look on his face but a slight gleam in his eye. "I am a merchant on the way to market. Underneath one arm I carry a live pig, and in that hand a washtub. Under the other arm I have a melon, and in that hand a live chicken.

"Even if I had a mind to commit such a bold act," he continued, "I could not do so for fear of losing my entire inventory."

"No, Julio," responded Jenny, without hesitation. "You could place the pig on the ground and put the washtub over him. Then you could put the melon on top to hold it in place. And then I could hold the chicken."

Jenny was a winner and was willing to take responsibility for her own actions. She did not use the language of noncommitment.

Resolve today to eliminate loser's elbow from your organization. When you are in a sales meeting or a one-on-one conversation and someone starts speaking in the language of noncommitment—"I'm not responsible," "It's somebody else's job"—simply extend your elbow out in any direction, snapping it quickly, and explain the principle of loser's elbow. Then they will begin to understand this all-important principle of winning in the game of work. We, as coaches, have the responsibility to establish the emotional and attitudinal climate of our team, our company, our business—and there should be no place for loser's elbow, the language of noncommitment.

WINNERS DON'T SEEK TO CHANGE THE RULES

Winners don't change the rules, they seek only to understand them well enough to win.

At the 1996 Summer Olympic Games in Atlanta, the United States women's gymnastics team was heading toward the gold medal when Kerri Strug, the team's last performer in the last event, severely sprained her ankle. Talk about bad timing. Here they are, on the verge of collecting America's first-ever women's team gymnastics gold medal, needing just one more vault to hold off the Russians and lock it up, and suddenly the athlete who's supposed to perform that vault is having a hard time standing up.

It was at this point of the competition, with an estimated billion people watching around the world, that Bela Karolyi, Strug's coach, marched over to the Russian coach and said, "OK, our girl's hurt. We'll count what she did yesterday, when both her ankles were healthy. Got to keep this thing fair."

You don't remember that? Of course you don't. That's not the way winners behave. Instead, Karolyi shouted out to his athlete, "Come on, Kerri, you can do it. This is what you've trained for."

Kerri got up and limped back to the head of the runway. She

had just seventy-five seconds to complete her vault. After another glance at her coach she set off, running. She vaulted high into the air, executed a twisting one-and-a-half somersault, and landed solidly on both feet. She even managed a kind of "take that!" smile in the direction of the judge before she lifted her aching ankle off the mat once she'd "stuck" her landing. Kerri Strug knew that the rules don't change, that it's your performance that you are judged on.

Think about all the people who are trying to change the rules today. They are trying so hard to make things fair and equal that they never get into the real game where they can win.

We will always have leaders and followers, winners and losers, people who add to and people who take away. A lot of things need changing, but winners don't try to change the rules in the middle of the game; they seek only to understand them well enough to win.

Jay Van Andel, one-time chairman of the board of the United States Chamber of Commerce, once said: "We are not going to help the caboose catch up to the engine by stopping the train." Certainly we need to seek change and improvement, but too many people are trying to change the rules for an easy shortcut or a free lunch so they can receive the benefits of winning without having to play the game.

WINNERS PAY THE PRICE—WILLINGLY—BECAUSE THEY KNOW IT'S A BARGAIN

How many times have you heard this one?

"If you want to be a winner, you've got to pay the price?" And they always say it as if they had just had a dill pickle.

"Pay the price, it's going to hurt."

"No pain, no gain."

"Take another ten laps. Don't stop when the blisters pop."

"Lift the bar until you can't lift it anymore, and then lift it one more time."

Losers pay a price, too, but winners pay it *willingly.*

Eric Heiden is a real winner. At age twenty-one, he won five gold medals in speed skating at the 1980 Lake Placid Winter Olympic Games for the best individual performance ever—a record that stands to this day. Heiden is from Wisconsin. His training schedule included starting on the university soccer team and then running the 289 steps up the ski-jump hill. Plus, he skated in those subzero winters wearing a thin racing suit.

But he didn't train outside all the time. He had a training room equipped with a stainless steel platform about seven and a half feet wide with a four-inch lip around the edge. In training for the Olympics he got on the platform and exercised four hours at a time, day after day, week after week, year after year. They showed it on television, and what kind of expression do you think was on Eric's face?

There was no agony, pain, or disappointment. Just a smile, the expression of a winner. And behind the camera, in full view, Eric could see a picture of the gold medals he was going to win. Winners pay the price willingly because they know it's a bargain. And when you concentrate on the end result, the obstacles melt away in the intensity of the preparation.

Winners are more willing to pay the price as the coach becomes more skilled at painting vivid pictures of the end results or benefits. Putting the *why* into our communication brings about incredible performances from the players.

WINNERS SET GOALS

Winning and goal setting are synonymous. You can't win unless you know what victory represents. There are a lot of losers who work just as hard as the people who win, but they never figure out when to stop and celebrate. But, most of all, winners are goal setters.

Tiger Woods came on the golf scene in the mid-1990s like a

hurricane unseen in thirty years. Winner of three U.S. Amateur championships, he was a "winner" from his first tee shot. Did he just fall there? No, of course not. Almost since birth, the goals had been set. For him at first, and then accepted by, embraced by, and internalized by Tiger himself. On the *Mike Douglas Show* at three years of age, hitting shots at eleven months, he woke up every morning to the press clippings of Jack Nicklaus and the other greats he would first emulate and then eclipse in his first professional season. Few before him and none since had won the first major they played as a professional. And how did he do it? "Huge goals, he has huge goals, and only when you have huge goals can you accomplish great things," was the quote from one of those who found themselves in that historic 1997 Masters competing for second place and being able to impact Tiger's victory only by their admiring applause on the eighteenth green. Could he win the Grand Slam, Masters, U.S. Open, British Open, and PGA championship in a single season? His response, "on paper it is possible!" And who among us is foolish enough to believe it is not also possible in his heart. Winners are goal setters, and more importantly, goal getters.

Winners are goal setters, and the rise or fall of every organization is based on the ability of individuals in those organizations to set and achieve goals. Setting a clear goal will give you more motivation than someone holding a gun to your head or a thousand-dollar bill in front of your nose.

Ted Ligety was called an overnight sensation when he became, at age twenty-one, the youngest American alpine skier to ever win an Olympic gold medal.

But Ligety was on skis when he was two years old and when he was in grade school he wrote that his goal was to be an Olympic champion. He attended summer school so he could have more time in the winter for training in the mountains near his home in Park City, Utah.

When it got dark he would continue to ski and race on the lighted runs. They had to drag him off the hill. He was never a sure thing. He wasn't even put on the U.S. national development team until he was eighteen. But he always had his goal. And at twenty-one, after spending most of his lifetime pursuing it, he became that overnight sensation. Goal setting is the strongest force in the world for human motivation.

But you don't have to be an Olympic athlete or a professional football player to make goals work. You don't have to start as a kid, either.

In his autobiography, Harland Sanders, founder of Kentucky Fried Chicken, tells about the Great Depression. He said he thoughtfully planned a scheme for kidnapping and holding for ransom the child of a wealthy neighbor to buy food. He was flat broke four times. He was cooking chicken in his wife's restaurant because he couldn't make it in the motel business.

The Colonel cooked his first piece of Kentucky Fried Chicken at 3900 South State Street in Salt Lake City when he was sixty-five years old. Then he left for a few weeks. When he came back the place had gone wild. Everybody wanted that Kentucky-fried chicken.

At seventy-two he sold out to John Y. Brown, the former governor of Kentucky and one-time owner of the Boston Celtics. The Colonel received $2 million plus $250,000 a year in personal-appearance contracts.

Harland Sanders has the most recognized face in the world, next to Mickey Mouse. At age eighty-eight he was asked if he had any more goals. "Yup," he said. "I've got three of them. Number one, I'd like to live twelve more years and become a centenarian. Second, at 100 I would like to take two years off, because I haven't had a vacation since I cooked that first piece of chicken, and I'm getting tired. Third, after I get off my vacation at 102, I'd like to come back with a new idea and make another major impact on American life." Leukemia took him at age ninety, so he never reached those last goals. Still, goal setting is the strongest force in the world for human motivation.

A little over 3 percent of the people in the United States are considered financially independent. Do you have any idea what minimum net worth is required to be included in that select category? A million dollars, perhaps? Actually a good guess.

According to the book *The Millionaire Next Door* there are approximately 3 percent of the households in the United States with net worth in excess of $1,000,000. And that net worth is accompanied by a minimum annual income just over $135,000 per year, with an average income of $260,000. That would place you in the top 3 percent of all American households.

Ten percent of the households have net worth between $350,000 and $1,000,000. They earn between $80,000 and $120,000 per year. These people are deemed by the reporters to be financially comfortable.

Sixty percent of the people in the United States barely make a living. Their net worth is tied up primarily in the homes they live in, and it is mostly offset with credit and debt.

Twenty-seven percent of the people need some form of outside support just to survive. It fluctuates depending on who's in the White House.

What do you think distinguishes the top two groups from the bottom two, other than the fact that the top two are where everyone wants to be? The top two groups are goal oriented, while those in the bottom group have few goals, if any. Still, the 3 percent group, on the average, outperforms the 10 percent group fifty to one. The average net worth of the 3 percent group is many times greater than the average net worth of the 10 percent group. Yet there are no demographic differences between the two groups—no significant differences in age, race, religion, education, sex, and parental wealth.

The big difference is that the people in the 3 percent group have prepared written goals with specific plans for reaching those goals. Not very many people are willing to do that.

Why don't people like to set goals? Why don't people like to write them down? Some people don't like to measure performance—fear of failure, perhaps. Some people are lazy. But look at what they are passing up. Rich people live longer and better and seem to be happier. And, contrary to all the publicity, the people in this group have fewer divorces.

Franklin D. Roosevelt constructed his plan for the presidency of the United States twenty years before he was elected. The world's greatest and most beautiful buildings, bridges, and airplanes are first created, in elaborate detail, on the drawing board before the first brick or piece of metal is set in place. Writing goals allows us to transform our dreams into a specific plan that can be shared with others for achievement. Written goals are not opinions or whims or wishes. Writing goals is the key step that turns dreams into reality. It makes the difference between losing and winning.

We must be the architects of our own lives. Who do you go to when you are preparing to build your dream house? That's correct, the architect. And why? Why would any of us spend the 6 to 8 percent of the total value of the house on the architect? In a $500,000 house, that extra $30,000 or $40,000 could make a substantial difference in amenities. Why then do we commit that portion of the budget to this discipline? Because the architect takes the hazy ideas in our minds and reduces them to written plans so that others can help in doing the work. Does it not make perfect sense that if this skill is important in the creation of a home that represents approximately five years of total annual income that we need the same skill in the way we live the remainder of our lives?

·eight·

Attitudes of Winners

If you are going to be a successful duck hunter, you must go where the ducks are.

PAUL "BEAR" BRYANT

In 1978, when I was just beginning to see the many parallels between sports and business, I decided to interview some real winners. I got on the phone and called Alabama. I wanted to talk to Paul "Bear" Bryant, who was then head football coach at the University of Alabama.

I just dialed the area code and asked for "The Bear." Immediately the operator put me through to this man who had become a legend in his own time. In 1982 the Alabama legislature met to pass an exception to its law of mandatory retirement at age seventy. The addendum stated that The Bear could work for the state of Alabama as long as he pleased. That's how much they thought of that man in Alabama. Bear Bryant passed away in 1983.

When I got him on the phone I asked him if he was a winner. He growled, "I won 307 football games. I won 88.7 percent of all the ball games I ever coached."

I got the message. He was specific. I thanked him for his time and hung up the phone.

Then I called the head football coach at a local state university, a major university with national recognition in many areas, thinking he too would know about winning. I asked him if he was a winner.

He said, "Chuck, you've got to understand something."

Right away I knew I was in trouble.

"You've got to understand," he said, "that I've got the seventh smallest budget in the conference. If I finish higher than seventh, I'm not doing bad."

I thought maybe he didn't hear me, so I repeated the question: "Coach, are you a winner?"

"Chuck," he said, "you've got to understand that they don't support football in this town the way they do down the highway (at the conference champion school)."

I thought I'd give him one more shot. I said, "Coach, are you a winner?"

He said, "Do you know how hard it is to get those kids from Southern California to come up here and play football?"

My conversation with the coach reminded me of a retail clothing store I did some work with. I asked the president of the company what he would most like us to do for him.

"I'd like to have you stop the weather reports," he said.

I didn't know what he was talking about and I asked him to explain. He did.

"I've got these eight retail stores out there," he said, "and every time I call up and ask how sales are, they give me the weather report. If I ask if everybody showed up for work, they say it's snowing and the people couldn't get in. Or the customers had to stay home because it's raining. Just stop the weather reports!"

What this manager really wanted was for me to get his employees looking at the scorecards and goals instead of making excuses for bad performance. He wanted specifics, not generalities. Winners are specific.

WINNERS PLAY THE ODDS

One time a bleeding-heart reporter was interviewing Willie Sutton, the famous bank robber. The reporter was trying to gain insights into the criminal mind in an effort to better understand criminal behavior.

"Willie, why do you rob banks?" asked the reporter in all sincerity.

"Because that's where the money is," responded Willie.

Like Willie, winners understand probabilities. They go where the money is. They understand the Pareto Principle. Pareto, history tells us, was an Italian sociologist who studied tax rolls and tax rates and concluded that 20 percent of the property owners paid 80 percent of the property taxes. I don't know what that discovery did for Mr. Pareto, but I know it is a hot subject in business circles. You and I know it as the 80–20 Principle.

I once had the opportunity to work with a communications firm that was leading in its market—they had it made. I remember one of their salesmen, a seven-year veteran, a man well past the middle of his life. He was the kind of person who's hard to motivate because he already has most of the material things he wants in life. He was the number-four producer in the sales network, one of those solid individuals you just build the company around. He was the good old boy.

As we began to meet, he was always saying that he was too busy for my goal-setting gimmicks. He had a lot of work to do, things that had to be attended to, and people to call on—hustle, hustle, hustle. My goal setting wouldn't work for him because I didn't understand his business and I didn't understand the market.

He was a hustler, a hard worker. He had a plan: he would go out and work hard, hope he sold a lot, try to develop new accounts, get that extra business, and make the goals. He knew he was really good. The commission checks just rolled in. He was typical—too typical.

I introduced him to the 80–20 Principle—that 20 percent of his accounts produced 80 percent of his business.

"Chuck," he responded, "you don't understand this business at all."

As we continued our debate, I asked him to consider the investment in my services his company had already made, and I asked him to try it my way, just once. I asked him to take his previous year's sales records and go back and calculate how much of his business came from each customer and to rank them according to dollars spent with him.

He reluctantly agreed to follow my suggestion and returned just a week later with a satisfied look on his face, as if he had proven something to somebody.

"You said that 20 percent of my accounts would be 80 percent of my volume," he said.

"That's true," I responded.

"You were wrong," he said. But along with that look of satisfied defiance, I noticed a little hint that he may have learned something as well.

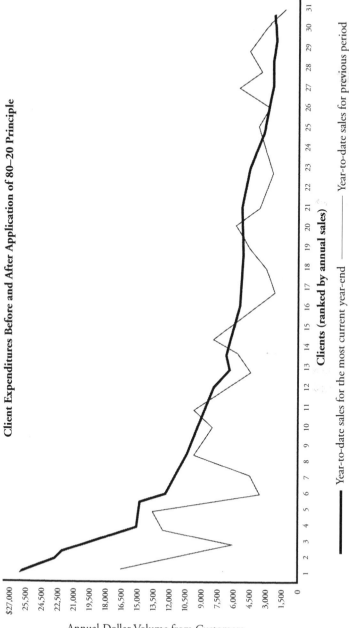

Client Expenditures Before and After Application of 80–20 Principle

Annual Dollar Volume from Customers

$27,000
25,500
24,500
22,500
21,000
19,500
18,000
16,500
15,000
13,500
12,000
10,500
9,000
7,500
6,000
4,500
3,000
1,500
0

1 2 3 4 5 6 7 8 9 10 11 12 13 14 15 16 17 18 19 20 21 22 23 24 25 26 27 28 29 30 31

Clients (ranked by annual sales)

Year-to-date sales for the most current year-end ——— Year-to-date sales for previous period

* Note the improvement in all the top 10 accounts, with only a slight decline in accounts 11 and 15.

"How far off was I?" I asked.

"The top nineteen accounts, out of a total of 104, accounted for 83 percent of my business," he said, as he and the rest of the people in the room began to laugh.

"I want you to know, too," he continued, "that another six of my accounts produced the next 13 percent of my volume, and that twenty-five of my 104 accounts produced 96 percent of all the dollar volume I did last year."

"How do you feel?" I said.

"Wonderfully embarrassed."

"What are you going to do now?"

"I'm going to take the bottom forty accounts," he said, "and lay them on the sales manager's desk with a note that I don't deserve to work with them."

He did that, and the sales manager was shocked and immediately created a draft pool to redistribute accounts to new salespeople.

The salesman said he was going to major on the majors. He laid out a schedule over the next ninety days to meet with each of his accounts in descending order from the largest to the smallest. The time that would have been spent on the forty accounts he didn't have anymore, he used to identify and penetrate into new business that had the potential to compete in size with his best clients.

Four months later he told me he had just received his largest commission check since coming to work for the company. He had paid off a couple of second mortgages on his different investment properties, and he and his wife were enjoying a lifestyle unparalleled in their history. An understanding of the 80–20 Principle had enabled him to major on the majors, thanks to a simple scorekeeping technique.

Incidentally, he came into my program with a goal to increase sales by 13 percent. Ninety days later he revised it to 47 percent, then exceeded that and achieved a 55 percent increase in sales the first twelve months after starting a tracking system. The tracking system enabled him to motivate himself without outside pressure, to realize more of his own untapped potential.

The 80–20 Principle can be graphically illustrated for any business or salesperson as shown on the chart on the preceding page.

Majoring on the majors can produce these same results for your team. The marketplace defines how the team is doing. Major on making the strong stronger.

In industrial sales accounts there is a fairly safe, yet aggressive application of the 80–20 Principle that can result in dramatic results when the customer base is reasonably constant.

First, take the 20 percent of your accounts that account for 80 percent of your business and establish a goal for a 25 percent increase in that group of accounts. If accomplished, this increase can replace all the business obtained from the other 80 percent of the accounts. Any business at all from the other 80 percent will be increased business. This is the first step.

The second step is to take the next 40 percent of your accounts that traditionally accounted for about 16 percent of your business and set a goal to double the business from this group of accounts. This is a reasonable, logical plan, giving you the opportunity to build a 32 percent increase into your sales and still generate excess accounts that are available for redistribution to young, aggressive new sales people.

I have had a lot of success, and fun, teaching companies how to manage the pool of leftover accounts. We have set up a system similar to the NFL draft, where the lowest producing salesperson gets first draft pick from the pool, the next to the lowest salesperson getting the second pick, and so on. At the end of the draft, the salespeople are given a short period for trading. Then, in thirty days, each salesperson is expected to turn in to the sales manager a written plan of attack for each of the new accounts. At the end of this process any leftover accounts are turned over to the inside order desk to become house accounts or to be part of a telemarketing program.

Frequently it's necessary to differentiate between types of productivity analyzed. Inventory, for example, can be subdivided into different items or groups of items with varying turnover rates. Again the 80–20 Principle can be applied. Often, 20 percent of the items in inventory account for 80 percent of the sales volume.

Several years ago I helped a paint distributor get his inventory under control. I asked him how he tracked individual products. He said he didn't need to because he had established a company goal to have everything in stock 100 percent of the time, a goal so often emphasized that it simply didn't need to be tracked.

Finally, after much discussion, he agreed to spend fifty dollars' worth of a clerk's time to measure the company's actual ability to have on hand the desired product 100 percent of the time. We discovered during the first week, in the middle of the prime selling season, that 17 percent of the orders couldn't be shipped because of insufficient inventory. The president was flabbergasted.

"We can't have this," he said. "It must have been an unusual week."

We agreed to continue the tracking, and in the second week 16 percent of the orders couldn't be shipped because of the insufficient inventory. The president was beginning to listen. He agreed to continue the tracking until we achieved the desired results.

Within two and a half months we had the number of unfillable orders down to 6 percent. But we weren't satisfied. The inventory was too large. And there was some question about the value of our measurements.

We acknowledged the 80–20 Principle and agreed that there

needed to be differentiation between different inventory items, with more emphasis where the greater problems existed. We divided the inventory into three groups. Exactly 20 percent of the items fell into group A, which comprised 78 percent of total sales. Management resolved to never be out of stock on these items. We tracked them separately from the other two groups.

Group B consisted of 40 percent of the items responsible for 17 percent of sales. We agreed that these were necessary items to stock, but not imperative for the success of the organization. Frequently these items were the same product as in group A, but in different-sized containers. Sometimes they were paints where the color was just a shade off the group-A color. Often substitutions could be made if these items were out of stock. We determined that with group-B items the company could maintain a higher risk of running out.

Group C, the bottom 40 percent of the inventory, accounted for less than 5 percent of total sales. The president was amazed that he had so much money tied up in such a small part of his business. It was obvious that the company could accept a much higher out-of-stock risk with items that made up such a small part of the business. We concluded that with many of the items it would be better to air freight them in than tie up so much capital in inventory.

We established criteria for each inventory level, measured by weeks on-hand. In group A we decided that in the peak season we would attempt to carry an eight-week supply. In group B we decided to carry a two-week supply, maintaining a six-week average for all inventory. For group C we maintained no safety level, just one item on the shelf to be reordered when it was sold.

We began to beef up orders for group-A items to get to the eight-week level, and we reduced orders for group-B and group-C items. As we finished the busy season, we had reduced the inventory from $290,000 to $165,000 and banked $115,000 of former operating capital, while maintaining a customer-order-satisfied record of 93 percent. By keeping score you can have your cake and eat it, too.

In business we often hear—and my father the grocer has repeated it many times—that we cannot afford to ignore any customer. Every one is important. Although this is true, applications of the 80–20 Principle occur so often and with such force that it cannot be ignored.

If you are going to hunt ducks, you must go where the ducks are. And if you are going to kill giants, you must spend your time in the beanstalks, not in the pea vines. After consulting in detail with thousands of businesses, I don't hesitate to say that there are applications of the 80–20 Principle in every business.

Losers refuse to face up to such facts. That is why they lose. But winners face up to what is really happening—they even keep track of it. That winning attitude gives them the knowledge they need to win.

·nine·

Results to Resources Ratio

If winning isn't important, why do we spend all that money on scoreboards?

CHUCK COONRADT

In business, one of the most effective measurement devices is return on investment. It may be expressed in several ways: return on assets, return on equity, return on net capital invested, or return on net assets. Return on investment measures the amount of profitability one can generate with certain assets, be they inventory, people, cash, real estate, or equipment. We do very well in using this measurement on an overall company level. We look at it annually—it's always in the annual report. And we may even evaluate it quarterly, but seldom more frequently than that.

There is a parallel in recreation and sports. We can use the term Results-to-Resources Ratio, or the RRR. In athletics—baseball, for example—there are several results-to-resources ratios. Batting championships are decided on the batting average, the relationship between the number of at-bats (resource), and the number of hits (result). The RRR for a league leader will be in the high .300s, perhaps over .375. One of the greatest batters in history by this measurement was Ted Williams, who batted .406 for an entire season. Batting average is an RRR.

In football we have an RRR for practically every member of the team. Offensive line coaches rate each player's performance on the number of times the block is effectively held long enough to permit the play to develop, be it a pass-blocking assignment or a running block. The number of opportunities or the number of plays in which a lineman blocks versus the number of times he holds the block for the required number of seconds reflect that RRR.

As we move into what are called the skill positions, those that come in contact with the ball, we have an even larger number of results-to-resources ratios. Receiver performance is measured in total receptions, receptions per game, yards per reception or game, number of games over a hundred yards, and total yardage for the season. In fact, in all sports, computers constantly measure results-to-resources for all of the players and generate beautiful computer graphics explaining those numbers to the fans over television.

In golf, the money becomes the most important measurement. Everybody knows how much the top golfers earn. But along with that we have expanded RRRs, including average strokes per round. We have a driving percentage, which is the number of drives placed in the fairway; the approach percentage, which is the number of approaches effectively delivered to the green from within 200 yards; and a putting percentage, or putts per round. These RRRs are measured in one-hundredths of strokes, even though the smallest increment of measurement in golf is one stroke. The experts recognize that if you put together all of the measured elements of the game consistently, with the right timing, you will come away with a victory.

The results-to-resources ratio is also essential in effectively managing a business. It's the key relationship between the stockholders and the management team. We must ask ourselves two questions: Why is it necessary? And why has it not been expanded further into management circles?

There are two reasons. First, we have never understood the obvious importance of the RRR in business. Second, we have never defined the fundamental way in which it is put together. Managers are inhibited or intimidated by this process. Let's set forth the method for constructing an RRR.

Divide a sheet of paper with one vertical line as in the next diagram. At the top of one side write "Resources." At the top of the other write "Results." For this example, let's use a controller in a medium-size organization who has a staff responsible for all the fundamental management accounting reports, payroll, accounts payable, accounts receivable, and so on. It might be easier to look at a mail sorter, salesperson, or lathe operator—but if we can do it for a controller, we can do it for anybody.

Now we may ask ourselves initially what her resources are. Some of the words come easily: time, subordinates, know-how, equipment, calculators, computers, peripherals. She also has a resource of space occupied by administrative people, space that cannot be assigned to sales or manufacturing or the productivity side of the business.

Results to Resources Ratio

Resources	Results
Time:	
Hours	
Minutes	

We must ask ourselves one major question: How do I measure the ingredients? When I write down "time," how do I measure it?

The easiest way, of course, is in hours and minutes. And so below "time" I write down the amount of time this person has available to her—forty hours a week. As a footnote, we may take the amount of time that she feels productive, the time she really feels she has to manage. (If you were measuring the time resources of an entrepreneur, you may pick the number of hours she spends away from her family.)

Now we go to subordinates' time. Again, it is measured in at least two ways. One is hours at work. You may look at an employee and write down his total departmental person-hours based on a forty-hour week, 4.3 weeks in a month, or 172 hours times the number of people on the staff. With a five-person department, he would have in excess of eight hundred hours plus the controller's hours on a monthly basis. A second way to measure the labor resource is in dollars of labor cost. We're beginning to define our resource.

Now, the machine time. We may look at that in dollars or in hours. We might look at the entire budget, including person-hours, space, and time in terms of an overall dollar cost for the business or any particular department.

As the manager begins to define resources, something becomes very apparent: resources in most organizations are easier to define than results. Selecting the right results is the essence of effective management by measurement.

Resources	Results
Time—800 person-hours Space—1,500 square feet Equipment—$7,000 a month	

Let's take the same approach on the right side of the chart. What results are we looking for from the controller? If you look at her job description, or the understanding she obtained in Accounting 101 in college, you will find words like: provide management with *timely, accurate,* and *complete* financial information to *profitably* conduct the affairs of the business organization.

Now, let's list each of the desired results: timely, accurate, and complete reporting. Behind each of these results we write a method of measuring them. If we are looking for accuracy, we might look at a percentage error factor. If we are looking for time lines, we might look at a variance between when reports were promised and when they were delivered. If we're looking for completeness, we can use either of the two previous statements.

Resources	Results
Timely—	Difference between regular project promise dates and delivery date.
Accurate—	1. Number of items done correctly before an error is made
	2. Number of times a report must be prepared to be accurate
Profitable —	1. Net profit for entire company
	2. Net or gross profit generated by an individual department

Now we want to identify the most expensive resource and the most valuable result and see if they can be combined. For example, we might look at this controller and her staff and conclude that the human element is, in fact, the most expensive resource we have. So let's underline that on the left-hand side of our chart. Next we'll go to the result side and ask ourselves the same question. What is our most valuable result? We might look, even though the controller is not in total control, at profit as the most important result we're looking for. We can then construct a preliminary ratio of net profit dollars per total department hours. *Net profit dollars per total department hours*—that's our Results-to-Resources Ratio.

Resources	Results
<u>People</u>	Timely
Space	Accurate
Equipment	<u>Profitable</u>

Net Profit per Department Hours

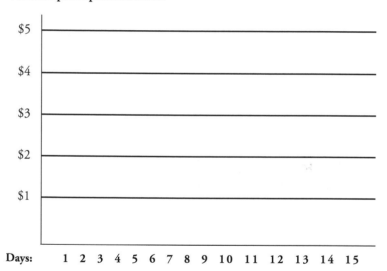

| Days: | 1 | 2 | 3 | 4 | 5 | 6 | 7 | 8 | 9 | 10 | 11 | 12 | 13 | 14 | 15 |

When you come up with a new RRR that becomes a measurement of someone's productivity or output, these questions invariably pop up: What does it mean? Even if we looked at it and found out what it said, what would it really mean? Is it worthwhile to keep track of it? We've never done this before. What are the measurements? Where do they go? Well, we recognize as managers that a number-one priority is to minimize the uncertainty on our team.

So, having introduced a new concept, we must expect to encounter some resistance. If we are able to do our research in such a fashion that we can look at historical data and assemble it in new terms before we necessarily expose our players to the information, we then have a tremendous opportunity to tell them what the new measurement means and reduce their fear and apprehension quickly.

For example, one of my clients recently went back and identified his net income per employee-hour for the last five years. He found change in the ratio from year to year of the magnitude on the following page.

With this historical perspective, the chairman of the board committed the human resources manager to provide a plan for subsequent staffing, not based on opinion, observation, or judgment, but on a measurement of a results-to-resources ratio.

The important concept here is to get the RRR to reflect accurately the philosophies and intent of the organization. For example, we might conclude that in a typical growing, developing organization, after the initial addition of computers and personnel to the accounting department, the relationship between total accounting department expenses and sales would begin to decline. Procedures would become routine as the company begins to grow. After all, it takes only a marginally greater amount of time to process twice the number of invoices. The input times are not doubled for orders that are twice as big. We need only one vice president controller. We will tend to fill in with lower wage-scale people. Our average hourly rate should come down with the passing of time. And so I think we could make a case for the fact that the RRR we call sales-per-administrative person-hour might be expected to rise over time.

Year	1	2	3	4	5
Profit increases	31%	27%	15%	11%	5%
Wage increases	9%	11%	14%	17%	18%
Net Gain in productivity per dollar paid	22%	18%	1%	(6%)	(14%)

Profit: _____

Wages: - - - - - - - - - - - -

Productivity: ▬▬▬▬▬▬

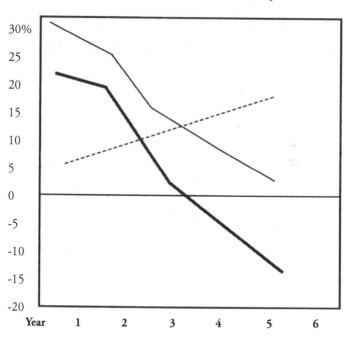

I know that if you track any company over a ten-year period, you will find that without measurement by management those costs have in fact not decreased but increased, and that the sales-per-administrative hour have gone down over time in spite of inflationary pressure to increase prices. We are, in most instances, doing less work with more people today than we were ten years ago.

Since a computer is absolutely essential—reducing turn-around time and making a contribution to the organization over the cost of that computer—there should be real savings when you add the cost of the new resource to the resource side of our chart.

Before you accuse me of unrelenting conservativism, let me point out that it is not my purpose to impose a direction on your business. If you wish to increase your administrative costs as a percentage of sales, that's your business and your right. My point is that you need to know what is happening, to know if you are winning or losing. Management must provide workers or supervisors with a realistic and clearly defined expectation so that they have a chance of knowing whether they are winning or losing. The purpose of the RRR is to do that very thing.

Included in the concept of a RRR is the *per*. Sales *per* man-hour. Yards *per* game. Yards *per* carry. The *per* triggers the relationship between results and resources.

Every professional has *pers*. Every member of my management team has them. Every member of yours will want to develop them.

A word of caution: the concept of measurement is sometimes regarded as punitive and must therefore be approached carefully and sold to the players as a benefit.

When salespeople are in trouble, they have to call their coach more often. When a business has financial problems, we may call in the auditors, who count clearly and frequently until we fix the problem. Once it is fixed, almost denying the power of measurement and frequent feedback, the auditors leave and take the measurement system with them, and we are again left on our own with less feedback than we had when we were in problem mode, somehow feeling that we should continue to muddle through until business goes bad again, knowing that the auditors will return.

How do you gain a commitment to measurability? How do you reach inside and turn that switch on? We'll discuss that more in the chapter on motivation, but let me suggest that there are some levels of involvement that can be developed.

I mentioned earlier the advantage of a historical perspective. Take, for example, an accountant's receivables. It is easy to go back and create a thirty-six-month time line showing the pattern of days of sales outstanding, as on page 130.

If the information is generated and processed by the players, you teach the players the formula. As they go back over the past eighteen months or so and generate their own calculations and their own graphs, the impression on them will be substantial, much better than if the graph is presented to them by someone else. It will be better than having them go dig out the information and having someone else graph it. If you want to understand something, do it yourself—touch it, chart it, study it. The self-administration of a management measurement program is the very best way to generate commitment to the process.

If you have a highly resistant subordinate player, or you're attempting to influence a peer level where your authority may be less than clearly defined, consider going back and constructing a graph and then sharing that information with the players who are responsible for that area of performance. It will give them a broader concept of the point you wish to make when expecting behavior change.

If people can be sold on keeping score, out of curiosity or in an effort to do something fun with their job, you have succeeded. *If you*

Accounts Receivable Days Outstanding

Accounts Receivable Days Outstanding

can, through motivational communication, provide them with the why in your thinking and share with them the importance of their participation, you will have a commitment that will last as long as you continue to reinforce it. The RRRs can be sold and merchandised.

An important part of the effective installation of a management measurement system is that the leadership must lead the way by example. So, before imposing the idea on your subordinates or simply handing a copy of this book to someone and wishing them well, look around your own field of play and determine what your RRRs are. Make several lists, several pages. Look for various combinations. Look for the resource that is most expensive and the result that is most desirable. Some examples are: number of smiles per day, number of transactions per employee labor hour, days of sales of inventory on hand, working days of billings outstanding in accounts receivable, average billing days deposited per month in the cash deposits area, number of phone calls made between successful appointments, number of presentations between sales. The list goes on and on. Be tough on yourself and you will be more effective with your people. Get behind the idea. Get involved in it and get interested in it, and you will find that you can be the coach, the leader, and the team captain we all want so much on our team.

You may not, on your first attempt, come up with a perfect measurement, but if you will begin, if you will have the courage to try it and watch closely your own results, you will be more capable of producing results in others.

·ten·

Picking Winners

Freedom is greatest when the boundaries are clearly defined.
CHUCK COONRADT

Every year before the NFL draft begins, the teams have a lot of data to study— years of college statistics and scouting reports that may go as far back as high school. They have numerous personal observations to back up the numerical data.

In business, most of us do not have that kind of information to help us pick winners for our team. It's easy to pay Shaquille O'Neal millions of dollars after he has proven himself, but it's a lot tougher to snatch an eighteen-year-old high school graduate coming out early and give him a lot of money in the expectation that a few years down the road he'll become a star performer. By contrast, in business we must interview and hire people we know little about, but whom we have the responsibility to discover, nurture, and turn to value the untapped potential. And in many cases, immediately.

How do you do it? Simple, although not easy! Look for the numbers, not the number of schools they attended. Look for results: the candidates' track records in similar positions. And most importantly, search for their willingness to be accountable and keep score in the new position.

In sports they always check the numbers. When a baseball club trades pitchers for hitters, or fielders for catchers, they don't worry about the personality or who the person went to high school with. They care about performance, statistics. The key to picking winners is to get as close to the attributes we listed in the chapter on winning as possible. And when you can't get numbers, you look for heart. And how do you do that?

First, *winners believe in themselves and see a relationship between past accomplishments and the future assignment.* They can't have this if the future assignment isn't clearly spelled out. Good feelings about past success must be transferred to the new assignment.

Sometimes a wise manager may recognize qualities in recruits beyond what the new employees can see in themselves. A coach of a college championship team, who later became defensive coordinator of a Super Bowl championship team once said, "All coaching is, is taking a player where he can't take himself."

As a general rule, your most likely winner is the person who can find a direct relationship between past successes and the new assignment. By the time some successful college basketball players reach the NCAA Final Four, they have lost only a dozen games in their careers, since grade school. You wouldn't hire a talented offensive lineman to play quarterback. You want someone who has had success that can be associated with the new assignment.

Second, *winners have commitment to the team's direction.* They see a direct relationship between the company's goals and their own individual goals. In sports, these are the players who can see a relationship between the hours and hours of practice and the few moments of glory and recognize that as a bargain.

Third, *you're looking for coachability.* For every recognized winner there is a coach in the background. Winners recognize that good coaches have knowledge and information beyond their own capabilities, and they are willing to assimilate this through the coach. They are open to the leadership of others. The great ones have mentors.

On the locker-room wall at Michigan State University there used to be a sign that said, "The difference between good and great is a little extra effort." The word *little* was emphasized.

The rewards in sports usually don't accurately represent the "little" differences between winners and those who finish second.

In 1995 Greg Norman was the top money winner on the PGA Tour with an average score of 69.06, earning $1,655,000. Number nine that year was Vijay Singh, averaging 69.92 and earning $1,108,000. Norman earned 50 percent more than Singh while averaging only eighty-six hundredths of a stroke better per round!

Each year on the PGA Golf Tour, the winners are ranked by total earnings. In 2004 Ernie Els finished second, winning a total of $5,787,225. Tom Lehman, who played in the same number of tournaments, with essentially the same equipment, won $1,343,277.

Is there a difference between Els and Lehman? One earned almost four and a half million dollars more than the other. But what about the difference in their play? Is Els really that much better than Lehman?

The PGA keeps track of the average strokes per round for all the tournament players. The final statistics show that in winning his $5,787,225, Ernie Els averaged 69.69 strokes for every eighteen holes of golf he played on the tour. Lehman averaged 69.97. That's right!

Twenty-eight hundredths of a stroke cost Tom Lehman $4,443,948 in winnings! Twenty-eight hundredths of a stroke in eighteen holes, the little extra effort, the difference between good and great.

In 2005, Jimmy Johnson won his third straight Coca Cola 600 Nascar race, by less than a car length, and one one-hundredth of a second over Bobby Labonte. No one remembers who was second in the previous two years. Each year in 16,000 miles of racing, each of thirty-six winners is determined by less than a quarter of a lap. One quarter of a lap is 1/2000th difference in performance.

In three Winter Olympic Games in 1988, 1992 and 1994, the great women's speed skater, Bonnie Blair, won three consecutive gold medals by fifty-six hundredths of a second—combined!

And talk about obscure second-place finishes! Do you remember Mark Spitz, who won seven gold medals in the Munich Olympics way back in 1972? It remains the most outstanding performance by an amateur athlete in the history of the Games; a mark many think will never be broken. Mark Spitz's largest winning margin to gain that worldwide acclaim and attention was less than two full seconds. Can you remember any of the swimmers who finished second behind Spitz? Truly the difference between good and great is just a little extra effort.

The famous 1978 Belmont Stakes race between Affirmed and Alydar was so close that it took the steward twenty minutes to determine that Affirmed had won the race—the eleventh horse in history to win racing's Triple Crown. The payoff and the fame difference between those two horses are incalculable. And so it goes throughout every field of endeavor, even in the company where you work.

As you look for winners for your company, and as you seek to establish a winning environment, think about the difference between winners and losers in baseball. A .200 hitter is moved about by managers about as often as they change their socks. A .300 hitter like

Ken Griffey, Jr. is so valuable that when he fights with his manager, can you guess who they fire?

The difference between a .300 hitter and a .200 hitter is one more hit in every ten trips to the plate. If you take the full count, it's one more hit in every sixty pitches. Look for the potential employee with the slight edge of excellence.

There are several excellent books on interviewing potential employees. I won't attempt to override that great body of knowledge in a few short lines, but let me emphasize that the hiring process must be the beginning of a coach-winner relationship. The great coaches are those who constantly seek to minimize uncertainty, and that begins in the hiring process in which you establish the field of play.

Many business managers when interviewing a prospective employee have no concept of what it means to set up the field of play. They go through meaningless routines, like going over the new person's resumé: "So you worked at Ford Motor Company. How're they doing?" or "You went to Clayton Valley High School. Did you know Kayla Nelson? Class of '01 too, I believe."

How many business managers waste time reading back the resumé to an applicant as if he or she didn't know what was on it, or as if they are trying to catch the person in a lie.

At my company, the field-of-play interview goes something like this: "Joan, here's what I've got to have done," I begin. "I would expect you as a member of our sales staff to do whatever you would have to do to get one of our senior staff people in front of a CEO in a closing situation at least once every five working days. And here's how we calculate that. We have in our company what we call 'mean length of time between closing presentations,' and I'm going to show you how to track that. Your first goal would be to go out and get one. I don't know if that would take a week or a month, but you would need to get one. The second goal would be to get the second in less time than it took for the first. Your third goal would be to get the third in less time than the average of the first two. Your fourth goal would be to continue to beat your average."

I have helped other companies adopt variations of this formula. I know of no other field of play that has worked better in getting new salespeople working productively. After explaining what is expected, I tell the salespeople I expect them to chart their progress on a chart similar to the one on the following page.

I tell the applicants what some of the best and worst performances were by other employees; then I ask them if they would perform in the field of play I have outlined.

I make it clear that their performance will be evaluated on how well they perform within the guidelines, not on personality, charm, appearance, sex, race, how they did at Ford Motor Company, or who they knew in high school.

Then I go into more detail on *how* they could get those closing appointments—the number of contacts that would result in at least one opening presentation every day, and how former employees have done, especially the best ones. When I'm finished, the applicants have a clear picture of the field of play, a way to measure their performance, the record book so they know what to shoot for, and a clear understanding of my expectations. At the conclusion of this interview, I assess their past winning behavior, their commitment to our team direction, and their willingness to learn, grow, and be coached. If these criteria match our needs, we have valuable candidates to become team members. That's the way it is in sports, and that's the way it must be in every business.

The selection process in sports is based on performance, but it's also based on planned obsolescence, planned over-hiring, and planned preparation for the vagaries of the human animal. Consider that every pro football team carries fifty-two players per team, or that

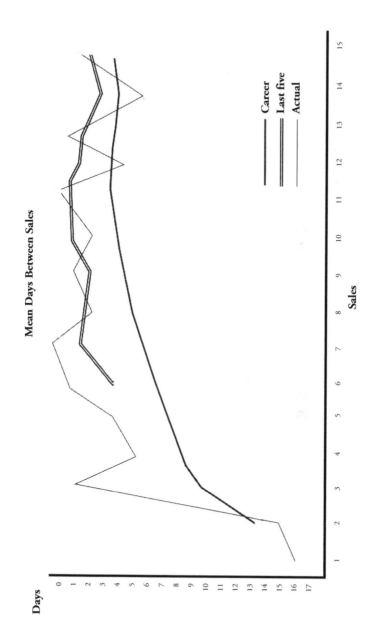

Mean Days Between Sales

Days

Sales

Career
Last five
Actual

the NFL has over fifteen hundred players on the league roster, and yet every year the league drafts another 400+ players who constitute possible candidates for replacement for additional growth in the business. Out of the 400, the league is prepared to add up to seventy-five new rookies and free agents. That's about 5 percent planned annual turnover. They do not commiserate about injuries or new contracts or competitive offers for other sports or the Canadian football league. They go about over-hiring based on their experience with turnover ratio. Recent statistics reveal that 99 percent of all the professional baseball players who have signed a contract since the beginning of the year have never appeared in a major-league game. There is a selection process in nature; there is a process that says that for every Olympic skating champion there are tens of thousands of young aspirants across the country looking for an opportunity to grow. A portion of them makes it to the nationals. One of those will become the Sarah Hughes or the Tara Lipinski or the Shizuka Arakawa of the next Olympiad. Why then do we so often ignore the obvious necessity to over-recruit, over-interview, and over-hire in order to find the very best people we're looking for.

When Reggie Bush entered the New Orleans Saints organization, the coach probably said something like this to him: "Reggie, here's what we expect from you. You'll be carrying the ball from twenty to thirty-five times a game. We expect you to average close to five yards a carry. We also expect you to decoy and block on this number of players, and catch so many passes, and sit on the bench when we're doing so and so. Any problem with that?"

Reggie might have responded, "Well, in college we didn't do it that way. I don't think I should have to block or catch anything but screen passes, and I don't want to sit on the bench. Besides, I've talked to one of the other running backs, and I think your expectations are unrealistic."

With a response like that, the coach would probably have said to Reggie, "That's fine. As I see it, you have only one of thirty-one decisions you need to make."

"What's that?"

"At which of the other thirty-one teams in the NFL would you like to play next year?"

As you move from hiring to coaching, the commitment to specificity must endure. I am amazed at the number of managers who express dissatisfaction with an employee's performance and then when that hopeful day arrives for the unsatisfactory employee to leave, one of the last things he or she is asked to do is train the replacement. Incredible! The manager abdicates the reins of leadership to someone whose work is unsatisfactory, enabling an undesirable situation to continue.

Managers must recognize that the joy or satisfaction in any experience is measured by the degree to which it meets or exceeds the expectations of the participant. Missed or unfulfilled expectations are the number-one cause of relationship failure. It is therefore imperative from the very beginning that you form the clearest possible expectations for an employee.

When I say earliest possible moment, I mean the very first day of work, or even earlier, in the recruiting process.

The athlete and the worker are both lost without a clear view of the field of play. Yet, what usually happens when new employees come aboard?

We bring them in the first morning and say, "Hi, how are you?" We sit them down at a desk and let another employee, frequently a mediocre performer, describe the field of play—an oftentimes warped picture—to the new employees.

Typically when you hire new employees you have their undivided attention until the first coffee break. They come in at 8 a.m. in a business suit, calling you Mr. Coonradt, eager to know what they can do for the company. What happens at the coffee break? They meet another employee, someone who's been around a long time and has a confused or warped picture of the field of play.

The new employees come back from the coffee break with the tie undone and the sleeves rolled up, and it's, "Chuck, baby. What's cookin'?" Too many managers turn over leadership responsibilities to the wrong people, abdicate the coach's role, and then spend the rest of their supervisory time with employees trying to keep them out of the terminal out-of-bounds area.

My recommendation is that when you hire new people, you don't let them out of your sight for the first forty-eight hours. Have them in all your meetings. Take them to lunch. Don't even let them go to the restroom unless you know they will be alone in there. There's only one chance for a first impression. Make sure new employees get a clear understanding of the correct field of play right from the beginning. It will save a lot of problems later on and could even make the difference between success or failure for an employee.

What many managers don't realize is that how people respond in an organization, and how they assess the organization in their minds, is primarily dependent on their relationship with the person to whom they report. When an employee comes aboard, the manager is in the driver's seat, receiving respect and appropriate responses from the new employee. That respect remains until expectations are not met. It's imperative that expectations be understood and clearly defined.

The need to establish the correct coach-player relationship can be seen in every training camp, regardless of professional or amateur, male or female athlete. The first thing a good coach does is establish the authority he/she will administer with the members of the team. It usually starts with the rules of the road, a list of acceptable and unacceptable behaviors that the coach expects from the team. They also outline the consequences of violations of these rules of the road: suspension, or being released from the team.

Why is this so important? Because it allows the coach to then concentrate on the behaviors he/she needs to develop in those team members. When the boundaries are clearly defined, as the team member may approach those boundaries, the coach can quietly and simply remind the player of where those boundaries exist, with a "warning track" discussion, and avoid disaster. If the coach does not establish those guidelines, along with the goals that specify how the player is to win and succeed, they have done an incomplete job of orientation, and will pay the price repeatedly for the lack of solid foundation.

It actually allows the coach to coach more gently, because consequences are clearly defined.

·eleven·

Coaching Winners to Greatness

All coaching is, is taking a player where he can't take himself.
BILL MCCARTNEY (COACH OF A COLLEGE CHAMPIONSHIP TEAM, WHO
LATER BECAME THE DEFENSIVE COORDINATOR OF A SUPER BOWL TEAM)

What is motivation? Drive, incentive, desire, go-power, something you need when you don't have it—like credit at the bank. Billions of dollars are spent on motivation every year. Look at all the pins, plaques, awards, prizes, and, of course, the jackets and blazers—red, blue, white, black, and gold.

What is motivation? If you split this word in half, the first word you have is "motive." And if you add one letter to the back half, you have "action." Motivation is a motive for action—a reason to do something.

Motivation is always present. It may be good, bad, or have no morality at all, but it is always there. It's happening, or not happening, now. It's not something you can buy in a box or bottle and put on a shelf.

There is no such thing as an unmotivated person. Teenagers who are too tired to mow the lawn on a Saturday afternoon are saving energy for a shower and a date! They are motivated, though not in the direction preferred by their parents. Everybody is motivated. Have you had a drink in the last twenty-four hours? You were motivated by thirst to do so. Have you slept in the last twenty-four hours? You were motivated by weariness to do it.

The big question is how to get more motivation in the areas we desire, how to get ourselves and those around us more motivated in business and professional pursuits. In order to know how to get more of it, we must first understand how it works.

There are three kinds of motivation. Fear is the most common form. Parents use it on children, and bosses on workers, all the time. When you have a donkey cart at the bottom of a hill, the fear motivator is the little man cracking the whip. Like most fear motivators, he is sitting down. The theory is simple, but it doesn't always work, at least not as well as it should. Sometimes the donkey kicks back or sits down. If the hill is steep enough and the load heavy, the donkey gets to a point where he would rather take a beating than continue. People do that too.

Sometimes salespeople get to a point where they would rather sit in the office and starve than get out and work. Most offices have people who are starving to death. The best thing you can do for them is fire them. People are self-determined. You've got to let them do what they want to do. If they want to starve, you can't stop them, but you don't need to pay them while they are doing it.

One of the big problems with fear motivation is that you need somebody with a whip to watch over every donkey. That's expensive. If you have six people sitting around doing the starving routine and you kick one, the other five say, "Yup, see how tough it is." But they still don't go out and do anything. And then the human relations manager will come by and get after you for kicking the person. You can't win with fear.

The next alternative is to use incentive motivation. You get a long stick, tie a carrot on the end, and hold it out in front of the donkey's nose. According to the theory, the donkey will look at the carrot and pull the wagon to the top of the hill. But there are five kinds of situations where the carrot won't work.

First is when the donkey is not hungry enough. Sometimes when you have a donkey that is content with fifteen hundred carrots a month and you put him in a job where he can earn three thousand carrots a month, he'll slow down his performance to catch up with his expectations and needs. He's not hungry.

This happens frequently in the real-estate industry. Take someone who is used to earning $2,000 a month and make him a real-estate salesperson. His boss tells him to go out and get a new listing every three days. He does it. Then the boss makes the biggest mistake in the world. He sells a house for the new person, and then compounds the mistake by taking the salesperson to the closing and paying him a $6,000 commission in one day. This usually happens his fourth or fifth week in the business. The salesman puts it in his checking account, which is now much bigger than his self-image. He can't get his self-image to go up, so he waits for his checking account to go down.

The second situation where a carrot won't work is when the carrot isn't big enough. The donkey looks ahead at the carrot, then back at the load in the cart, then up at the steepness of the hill, and thinks, "If you think I'm going to pull this load up that hill for one lousy carrot . . ."

The third problem with carrots occurs when the road is too steep. You cannot ask people to do more than they are able. Sometimes taking a class, learning new skills, or gaining more product knowledge will change the situation.

Fourth, carrots won't work when the load is too heavy. This occurs when somebody says, "I know I can make a lot of money in this business, but do you know how many people I have to call on to make a sale?"

The fifth I discovered quite by accident. I was giving a lecture on motivation, and a woman in the back stood up and asked, "Chuck, what do you do if the donkey doesn't like carrots?" I wasn't prepared for that question. It stopped me dead in my tracks, and I started thinking about it.

It occurred to me that the woman had put me onto one of the fundamental problems of incentive motivation. Not long after that experience I was sitting in the back row at a sales meeting when the vice president of the company showed the salespeople a beautiful television. It was to be presented to the top salesperson that month.

I was sitting next to two salespeople who had been around a long time. One of them poked the other and said, "Big deal, it's worth maybe $2,000. If I won, I would have to spend $4,000 to redo the family room just to make the decor right again." The salesperson thought that $2,000 carrot would cost nearly $4,000 to accept. She didn't like the carrot.

Another bad-carrot situation occurs when the executive says, "Work hard and we'll make you a manager."

The worker thinks, "Hmmm, manager. That's somebody who works 30 percent longer hours for 10 percent more money with three times the heart-attack rate and six times the divorce rate. I don't like your carrot." He'll slow down his performance just short of the prize. If you're going to use carrots, make sure the donkey likes them.

Whereas donkeys may respond to whips and carrots, people don't. People respond best to their own goals, if they have them. You don't need to treat people like donkeys if you understand goal striving. Reaching goals is a form of winning. People like to win. People who are trying to win by reaching clearly defined goals don't necessarily need carrots or whips. Winning is its own reward.

Remember, there is no such thing as an unmotivated person. Goal setting harnesses that motivation and channels it in the right direction. Through proper goal-setting techniques discussed in chapter 2, a person's desires, wants, and needs can be directed into purposeful activity.

The third and most effective form of motivation, self-motivation, takes place when people are allowed to choose their own rewards, set their own goals, and decide how they will accomplish those goals. People can be highly motivated in sports because they know nobody is going to change the rules or the boundaries in the middle of the game. Athletes can train and condition with all their heart, knowing that the rules or boundaries are not going to change. In recreation, the rules are clear by which I exchange my talents, abilities, and energy for the things I want to have. Unfortunately this is frequently not the case in business, and that is why in most cases people will pay for the privilege of working harder at play than they will work when they are paid. Motivation, then, the motive for action, is the trade between what I want and what I am willing to give for it.

Consider a balance beam, or a teeter-totter. Keep in mind that motivation is a *motive* for *action*. On the left side you have the weight or intensity of the motive. On the right side you have the weight or difficulty of the *action*.

MOTIVE   ACTION

▲

If I offer you a thousand dollars to call me Mr. Coonradt instead of Chuck, you will be motivated to obey, very quickly. A thousand dollars is a strong *motive*, while calling me Mr. Coonradt is an easy *action*. The thousand dollars will quickly motivate you to comply.

If I handed you a quarter in an attempt to get you to run ten miles with a fifty-pound pack on your back, you would think I was crazy. In this case the *action* far outweighs the *motive*, so nothing happens. *The key to motivation is providing motives that outweigh the desired actions.*

The relationship between *motive* and *action* is illustrated perfectly in a holdup that took place in the Old West. A homesteader and his wife were driving their wagon to town when a bandit jumped out of the bushes pointing a six-shooter at them and ordered the man to step down. He obeyed.

"Can you dance?" said the bandit to the man.

"No," responded the frightened farmer.

"We'll see," said the gunman. Then he fired three shots beneath the man's feet. The man danced and the outlaw laughed.

"Can your mule dance?" asked the gunman when the dust had settled.

"No," responded the frightened farmer.

"We'll see," said the gunman. Then he fired three shots beneath the poor animal's feet. The mule reared up and jerked the wagon about, frightening the woman.

The outlaw laughed again, until the woman reached under the seat, pulled out a double-barreled shotgun, and pointed it at the gunman.

"Boy," she said, "Is that a six-shooter in your hand?"

"Yes, ma'am," said the startled outlaw, beginning to wish he were somewhere else, realizing he had fired all six shots.

"Son," she continued, "have you ever kissed a mule?"

"No, ma'am," he said, looking up into the barrels of the shotgun, "but I'm looking forward to the privilege with great anticipation."

Whenever the motive outweighs the action you are going to get results. Everybody in the world has a balance beam in his head. Motivation is simply the process of piling things on the motive side until movement occurs and the action gets off the ground.

The bottom line in motivation is getting the balance beam to move. If you are a fear motivator and nothing is moving, you get a bigger whip. A shotgun at five feet is more effective than a pistol at a thousand yards. The problem is application. You can kick people out of the office, but you can't be with them every minute to make sure they are working. You can't afford a supervisor with a whip to oversee every worker.

If you are an incentive motivator and nothing is happening, you get a bigger carrot. But in a time of shrinking profit margins, you can't really afford bigger and bigger carrots. It would be nice to give everyone a $100,000 a year guarantee with twelve weeks paid vacation, but most companies would go broke offering that big a carrot. And sometimes you run into workers who don't want carrots.

So how do you get more motivation without investing in a bigger whip and more carrots? The key to successful motivation is individual involvement. That means tying the individual goals of your people to the goals of the business. To win at work, you create a methodology where people and the business are closely linked to grow together with common or compatible goals. In order for this to happen, you must recognize the following factors:

1. *WIIFM—What's in it for me?* A vital question all employees have on their mind when coming to work each morning is "What's in it for me?" Anytime people run into a new situation where they're going to be asked to perform, they've got this question: "What's in it for me?" Sometimes the question isn't verbalized because employees don't want the boss to think they are selfish people, troublemakers, or bad employees. Still, the question is there, and a smart manager will recognize it.

2. *WSI—Why should I?* Children ask "Why should I?" a lot, at least until they hear the nonanswer "Because I said so" so many times that they give up asking. Parents give this nonanswer because they don't know or are too lazy to figure out the real answer. They would be better off saying, "I don't know."

When people ask you with their mouth or their eyes (not all questions are asked with the mouth) "Why should I?" or "What's in it for me?" they are attempting to become self-motivated.

They are saying, "Manager, my beam's not tilted yet." "I haven't decided to go." "Help me out." "Let me understand more." "Tell me again." "Motivate me!"

There's something about the way people are put together that makes it almost impossible for them to do something until they understand why. Have you ever been in a situation where somebody asked you to do something new or unexpected without telling you why? Remember how hard it was to do it, if you did it at all?

I was working in the purchasing department of a company once when the president came in and said, "Would you look at the Barker account?"

"Sure," I said. "What am I looking for?"

"Just look at it," he said.

"Why?" I asked.

"Never mind. I just want you to go through every invoice that we've had from them for the last year."

"What am I looking for?" I repeated.

"I can't tell you. Just look at it."

I admit this is an extreme case, but it really happened. If the manager had said he suspected that somebody was stealing from us or that a purchasing agent was on the take, I could have waded into the project with a purpose. But I didn't know what he wanted. It took me three hours to get sufficiently motivated to go through the file. I did the job because he told me to do it, not because I understood what was to be accomplished. There was little self-motivation to achieve anything. Then when I was finished, he had the nerve to ask me to give him an analysis of what I had found.

There was a new husband who didn't know why his bride cut both ends off the ham as she prepared for their first Easter dinner. He asked her why. She didn't know, only that she had learned it from her mother. Later, when the mother arrived for dinner, the young husband asked her why she and her daughter cut the ends off of ham. The mother answered that she didn't know why, only that she had learned it from her mother, who would soon arrive to share the dinner with them.

When the grandmother didn't know why either, the young husband was so beside himself with curiosity that he got into his car and drove down to the rest home to ask the great-grandmother why she cut both ends off of hams.

The old lady was almost too feeble to speak, but when she finally understood the question, she explained that when she was a little girl, ovens were so small and hams so big that it was usually necessary to cut the ends off in order to get the hams into the oven. Consider all the wasted ham because nobody bothered to ask why.

3. *MMFI—Make me feel important!* A colleague of mine once doing some industrial research for a manufacturing company where he was trying to measure morale and attitudes. He interviewed people involved in various stages of the manufacturing process. In one area people were gluing what appeared to be pieces of white plastic onto pieces of hardwood, a very tedious and boring task. My friend went up to the first worker and asked, "How do you like your job?"

The man said it was a crummy job.

"What are you doing?" my friend asked.

"I'm putting these white things on these hard blocks."

"How do you like the company?"

"I don't," the man said.

"How do you like the benefits?"

"Who cares? They're not so great."

The researcher got similar responses from the next four or five workers. Then he came to a little old lady with her white hair tied up in a bun. She was whistling. The production charts showed that her production rate was 50 percent above the average.

"How do you like the company?" he asked.

"It's a great place to work," she responded. "Best job I ever had."

"How do you like the benefits?"

"They're super."

"How do you like your boss?"

"She's great."

"By the way," asked the interviewer. "What do you do?"

"I make pianos."

What she had figured out was that she was assembling piano keys. She knew that the fingers of a master or the hands of an inquiring child were going to use her keys to bring joy to themselves and others. She felt important about what she was doing, and she was motivated by that feeling of importance.

4. *Different strokes for different folks.* Mao Tse-Tung knew how to motivate people. He went in with a small band of Chinese communists and took control of China away from Chiang Kai-shek, who wanted democracy. By our standards Chiang Kai-shek was right and had the best interests of the people at heart, but while he preached democracy and freedom, Mao Tse-Tung was promising food, clothing, and shelter—what the people wanted and needed most at the time. Mao won. He had the uncanny ability to match the motives of his followers to the things he wanted accomplished. Great motivators can get a group of people to accomplish a single objective for a variety of individual reasons.

Think about the person in your office who is most in need of motivation. For an eye-opening experience, try filling out the form on page 156. Do you know the person's spouse's name? Do you know the age and primary activities of his or her kids? What hobbies does this person have? How involved is the person in these hobbies? Do you know where this person would like to be in your company in three years? Does your assessment agree with that? Do you know what this person's net worth is and what he or she would like it to be? If you went out of business, what would this person do to make a living?

By now you're probably beginning to feel a little inadequate,

EMPLOYEE AWARENESS QUESTIONNAIRE

How well do you know your people? Think of a subordinate or someone with whom you have less than an ideal motivational relationship. How well would you be able to answer these questions about them?

1. Name of employee's spouse or significant other.
2. Ages and first names of children.
3. What does he/she like to do off the job?
   - List three favorite nonwork activities.
   - Do you know his/her level of performance in each of these areas?
   - Do you know about awards or special recognition the person has received?
4. Name one thing each of his/her children is good at.
5. What does he/she think his/her next position in the company will be?
   - In his/her mind how soon will he/she be ready to accept it?
   - How closely does this agree with your assessment?
6. Do you know what he/she would do if the company went out of business?
7. Where does this person like to invest money?
8. What are the person's three greatest fears?

and I'm not even halfway through my list of questions. The point I am making is that *nobody can motivate a stranger with consistency.* Your ability to motivate people is directly related to how well you know them and how well you're able to match company goals with their needs and desires. You need to know as much as possible about the people you want to motivate.

And the reverse is true, too. They need to know as much as possible about you, the manager, and the company, too. *Nobody can do what you do unless they know what you know.* You cannot expect people to think the way you think unless they have the information you have.

A typical example is the boss who receives what he considers a bad profit-and-loss statement, gets mad, stuffs it in the drawer so nobody will see it, and then walks around with a scowl on his face for an entire month, hoping it will be better next time. He walks up to somebody taking an extra three minutes on a coffee break and says, "Don't you understand how much trouble we're in around here?" The employee says, "No." And the boss decides the employee is irresponsible and doesn't care.

If you want to get more self-motivation in people, get to know them better. If someone in your office is worried about getting bread on the table next week, you must know about it. If you've got someone with a $10,000 balloon payment due on a piece of real estate next month, you must know about that, too. Know what your people need and let them see that you and your organization offer a way for them to get it. They may not stay with you forever, but they'll perform better while they do.

·twelve·

Winning at the Game of Work

Everyday, everybody needs to know if they are winning or losing.

CHUCK COONRADT

Following are some real examples of companies taking the motivating principles of athletics and applying them in the business world. As you read these examples, think of ways to apply these principles to your own business.

CASH FLOW AT A RETAIL LUMBER YARD

On one occasion I was called in by a retail lumber company with three locations. The company was about to sell its best piece of real estate in an effort to improve cash flow. It had owned that piece of property for over thirty years, and the transfer fees and taxes would take a huge chunk of the money. They called me in for a "second opinion" before taking the plunge.

Since I believe there is no such thing as a cash-flow problem, my initial investigation uncovered what appeared to be a slackening of credit control and, more serious, a loosening up in purchasing controls affecting inventory turnover.

I recommended a twenty-four-month historical review of receivables and inventory. For the receivable measurement, I selected working days of credit sales outstanding and unpaid. This was arrived at as follows:

$$\frac{\text{Last 90 days' credit sales}}{\text{66 working days}} = \text{Average daily credit sales outstanding}$$

$$\frac{\text{Current period ending accounts receivable balance}}{\text{Average daily credit sales outstanding}} = \text{Working days of credit sales uncollected}$$

For the inventory we measured the weeks of inventory on hand.

$$\frac{\text{Last 13 weeks sales} \times \text{cost of goods sold percent}}{13} = \text{Average weekly cost of goods sold in dollars}$$

$$\frac{\text{Period ending inventory}}{\text{Average weekly cost of goods sold in dollars}} = \text{Weeks of inventory on hand}$$

These measurements were not very unusual, but they are excellent results-to-resources ratios.

We found that the working days of credit sales outstanding and unpaid had grown from a low of forty-three days to a high at the present time of sixty-seven days. That increase in twenty-four days of sales outstanding tied up just under a quarter of a million dollars of operating capital.

Our findings in the inventory area were even more remarkable. In a previous year's peak selling time of optimum turnover, the inventory had been reduced to the equivalent of 8.3 weeks of inventory on hand. No one could recall that there had been any unusual problems in filling orders, no increase in out-of-stock items, no increase in unhappy customers. The inventory, however, had been allowed to grow to 16.7 weeks in stock. The additional seven weeks of inventory tied up an additional $200,000 of operating capital. In just two areas, the introduction of scorekeeping—of keeping historical measurements—uncovered the opportunity to recover almost half a million dollars!

I recommended to management that they hold up on the sale of the real estate and get to work on the receivables and inventory. Thirteen weeks later receivables had been reduced to fifty-three (from sixty-seven) days outstanding, releasing $150,000 in working capital. Eighteen weeks later the inventory level was back to twelve weeks, releasing an additional $100,000 of operating capital. It was no longer necessary to sell the piece of real estate.

Let me emphasize that I am not talking about magic techniques to swamp the lucky executive with fistfuls of cash, though I have witnessed some seemingly miraculous results when proper scorekeeping methods were implemented. What I am talking about is players or competitors gaining an increased awareness of each opportunity to score.

Charting measurements over time, sometimes called a historical review, can magnify the understanding of measurement information many times.

But don't make the mistake of oversimplifying the problem. A golf course may be seventy-two hundred yards long with a par of seventy-two strokes. You may score par by averaging a hundred yards per stroke. The hundred-yard drives are a cinch, but what about the hundred-yard putts? Only by accurate scorekeeping and measurement of every part of the game do you improve each part of the game and come out a winner. Your drives will go well over one hundred yards, and your putts will never get close to the hundred-yard mark, but as you keep score on each part of the game, your averages will improve. The same principle applies in business.

INCREASED PROFITABILITY FOR A COMMUNICATIONS FIRM

Sometimes it's important to spend time getting the rules straight before starting to play. I was involved in such an opportunity. A public communications company called me in to help with budget plans for the new year. The firm had been languishing for years in a rather flat but still acceptable profit picture. Their operating profit had been bouncing between $1.4 and $1.9 million a year for four years. In the most recent year, it had dropped to $1.7 million.

It was September, and the CEO called me in to see if I could help get their fall budget and planning session off to a better start.

In our preliminary discussions, he discussed what the experts were saying about the stock market, what he thought were the plans of the competition for the coming year, the relationship with the holding company, and a dozen other irrelevant items used in previous years to get the budgeting process underway. It became clear to me that we needed to clarify the rules before the game began.

I asked him what kind of profit picture he would like for the new year. He responded by saying that the best they had ever done was $2.25 million.

"Would you like that again next year?" I asked.

"I don't know," he said. "I haven't finished studying all the economic predictions." He also indicated a string of unprofitable Januarys due to the fact that the budgeting for the new year, which was started in September, was never finished by January.

"Would you like to earn that much?" I persisted, realizing that his own will was among the most important factors in that company's profit planning.

"Yes," he finally said. "I believe I'd like to take a shot at it." And so we outlined a $2.25 million operating plan.

"What percentage of your profit comes from your major operating division?" I asked, and he said 86 percent had been the traditional contribution of the major division. We assigned 86 percent of the profit to the flagship division.

"Is that fair?" he asked.

"Do you believe it is?" I responded.

"I do," he said.

The next division accounted for just under 10 percent, so we rounded its share up to 10 percent, and the third division accounted for 4 percent. We allocated 100 percent of the corporate profit goal based on the historical percentage of revenue contribution. The CEO then mentioned all the other areas of responsibility that consumed various amounts of his budget. We agreed after a brief discussion that those areas would be subordinated to the three profit-making divisions and would not be discussed further until the plans for the profit-producing divisions had been established.

Safely convinced in my own mind that he and I were in accord, I left him that Friday afternoon looking forward to a Monday morning group meeting with the division heads.

At the Monday meeting he said, "Gentlemen, I've prepared the budget, and I'm going to ask you to meet some very simple requirements."

He then presented each of the division heads with an envelope containing the total net dollars of operating profit expected from each division. After the initial negative reactions, the managers went back to their offices and in half the normal time prepared operating plans that would get the CEO the amount of profit he asked for. The operating plans were finished by Thanksgiving, whereas in previous years they had not been finished before the end of the year. Though that initial meeting was tense, it was as it should have been: the CEO communicated clearly with his top managers, telling them exactly what he expected from them.

The company did not achieve the $2.25 million goal that year. It achieved $3.4 million, due mostly to two things. One, the early completion of the operating plans enabled the divisions to be off and running by the first of the year, whereas in previous years the plans hadn't been agreed upon until the end of January. Two, the general manager of the flagship division used his imagination to create one of the greatest customer incentive programs in the company's history. He said he knew what was expected, and because of that he went beyond the set budget. That year the meetings focused on profit and growth rather than on the usual nitpicking about expenses. With the profit goals clearly established at the outset, many of the negative, unnecessary activities were pushed aside. The managers loved the new system. They had clearly defined goals and a way to win. The leadership had come from the top. It was specific, direct, and intense.

The CEO later confessed to me that he didn't sleep well the Sunday night before that meeting, and that the weekend had been one of the most miserable of his entire life. When we met fifteen months ago he rejected my suggestion of a minimum 15 percent annual increase as being too tough and unrealistic. As we laughed about it over a record profit-and-loss statement, he told me that his profit goal for the coming year was $4.4 million.

IMPROVING MAINTENANCE FOR A TRUCKING FIRM

I was called into a $10 million a year trucking company to work on maintenance problems. First, we measured maintenance costs (labor and parts) as a percentage of total billings. Although this measurement was nearly twice the national average for similar firms, the measurements didn't show any dramatic fluctuations, so they were not very useful. We didn't have anything to compare the measurements against.

So we devised a nonstandard measurement—the average miles between breakdowns. We borrowed this idea from the U.S. Defense Department, which for years has been measuring the time between failures of its defense systems. We did the same thing with the trucks.

It was a self-administered scorekeeping system with the mechanics taking readings from the odometers of each truck when there was a breakdown. Routine maintenance and servicing were not included.

The mechanics or the supervisors of maintenance in each of the garage facilities built their own scorecard for each vehicle in their care. It was very simple, not cumbersome at all. The person in charge would simply subtract the odometer reading from the reading at the previous breakdown to get the miles between breakdowns.

Once the system was operational, we discovered one service terminal that needed immediate attention—its trucks were averaging only 750 miles between breakdowns. For the first time the company had an accurate record of how the various repair facilities were doing in comparison to each other. The system also enabled us to compare the service records of trucks from different manufacturers. We could also compare parts performance—spark plugs, axles, tires, and so on.

As a result of the new miles-between-breakdown measurement, the company increased the rotation frequency of vehicles and reduced overall transportation repair costs by 1.2 percent of sales. In that $10 million company, that resulted in an annual savings of $125,000.

IMPROVING THE CUSTOMER'S OPPORTUNITY TO GIVE YOU MONEY

I was called in to consult with a company that built custom overhead cranes for materials handling. As I began the investigation, I took a look at receivables, as I always do. Although receivables are normally updated monthly, they must be watched daily.

The standard way to track receivables is an aging report—dividing the money owed you into thirty-, sixty-, and ninety-day blocks. The aging report shows what percentage of the money owed you falls into each of the categories. When you confront the average collections manager on the status of receivables, he or she will give you some evasive rhetoric about percentage—that it is up 2 percent or down 2 percent, and that the total amount over ninety days is X. Good information, but you don't know where you are headed. You don't know if the situation is really getting better or worse.

The first measurement I added for the crane company was the number of days of business outstanding—the amount of business done in the last ninety days that they had not been paid for. This measurement is concise, flexible, and easily measured, and it gives rapid feedback. It tells you how good you are at getting the money owed you and if you are getting better or worse at collecting it.

As we began to track the number of days of business outstanding, we quickly recognized the company had a real problem with receivables. The number of days of business outstanding was approaching ninety.

As we began to discuss how the problem might be corrected, a casual slip of the tongue caught my immediate attention. Someone said, "I'll bet if we could get our invoices out faster, we'd get paid better."

"Tell me more," I said. "How long does it take now?"

What I heard was altogether too typical, an observation management response—a lot of talk about one invoice here, another there, two that had this or that problem. People involved in management by observation always cite the examples that reinforce their personal point of view. It was evident that nobody really knew how soon the invoices were sent out. No measurement existed.

I set up a simple scorecard to be completed by the invoice clerk under the direction of the controller. They began to identify and track the number of days required from job completion date until the invoice was in the mail to the customer.

On the first batch of twenty invoices, the average processing time was thirteen working days. The process of checking against the bid, auditing, price checking, and double-checking was causing a full month's delay in the customer's opportunity to pay.

Of course, the customer is never eager to pay, regardless of when the bill comes. But we decided the money would come faster if the invoices were sent out sooner, closer to the work completion dates. We also reasoned that most of the customers paid in some kind of billing cycle and that if we could get invoices to them sooner, we'd increase our chances of catching an earlier cycle.

The scorecard told us the invoicing performance was not up to our expectations. Armed with that information the controller began to explore the causes of the slow invoicing and how the situation might be corrected. Using additional scorecarding, he began to study the invoicing process, uncovering the bottlenecks. One by one he identified the problem areas and began to chip away at them. Within six weeks the average number of working days to produce an invoice to the customer had gone from thirteen down to three. We had eliminated almost two weeks out of the time required to get the invoice to the customer. Within six weeks we saw a noticeable improvement in collections.

CONTROLLING SEASONAL UNPROFITABILITY
IN A BOTTLING COMPANY

Another great example of using scorekeeping to bring seasonal fluctuations under control occurred in a small bottling company. They retained my services during a marginal profit year in an effort to curtail losses after the first of the year. The company traditionally had strong sales and profitability during the summer and fall months, peaking at the holiday season. After the first of the year, however, the company always entered a period of thirty to ninety days in the red.

In selecting a results-to-resources ratio, we identified two items that did not fluctuate with inflation, costs, or economy. The sales manager began to track each route or truck on the basis of cases delivered per gallons of fuel consumed by the truck. Adjustments were made for propane and diesel vehicles, and also for flatbed and gooseneck trailers. Almost immediately there was an increase for the first time in its history; the company operated in the black during January and February. When management saw this working, they introduced a cases-per-mile scorecard for their routes that enabled them to decrease labor costs in accordance with seasonal drops in sales. This one measurement alone enabled the company to reduce delivery costs by 15 percent with no appreciable decrease in sales revenues.

SHIFTING THE EMPHASIS FROM PEOPLE TO DOLLARS FOR THE MARCH OF DIMES

One of my clients was the volunteer supervisor of a March of Dimes telethon. The most money the group had ever raised was $78,000. In the past the goals of the person in charge had been measured in number of people contacted and other activities related to the fund-raising process.

We implemented a new program in which the emphasis was shifted from people contacted to dollars raised. We set up a tracking system based on performance in past years. The measurement system had the ability to update the progress hourly during the telethon.

With the new system in place, a goal of $100,000 was set, $22,000 higher than any amount previously raised. That first year they raised $110,000. Within three years the telethon was raising more than $200,000 a year.

EVEN WASTE CAN BE MEASURED

A fencing company asked me to help improve its overall productivity. The first thing we did was set up a noninflationary measurement for the entire company. We charted pounds of product per person-hour. We included management and clerical employees as well as production workers in the measurement. We started out at 127 pounds per person-hour, and after four months productivity had increased to 196 pounds per person-hour.

As we implemented the tracking system, it was necessary to devise several intermediate scorecards. One of the greatest challenges was keeping track of the scrap produced when six- and eight-gauge galvanized wire was drawn into nine- and eleven-gauge wire to be made into basket-weave fencing. The supervisor in charge of this drawing operation had no idea whether he was winning or losing. His goal seemed to be to minimize losses in a situation where dies would wear out and the gauge was inconsistent most of the time. Very little was ever right about the operation. When the operation was at peak performance, two nine-cubic-yard dumpsters were filled daily with scrap from broken dies, broken runs, operator error, and variety of other causes. The president of the organization was well aware that the company was spending thousands of dollars a month in hauling costs alone to dispose of the scrap wire.

At the suggestion of one of my associates, the company installed a device to weigh the scrap and provide immediate feedback to the operator. It was soon discovered that some of the operators were more wasteful than others, that some were not suited for that particular job. These were transferred or fired. Within six weeks of the installation of the weighing device, the amount of waste had an almost 80 percent reduction. Thus, there was an increased amount of wire going into finished galvanized fencing. And the scrap disposal costs were cut by $40,000 a year.

A SIMPLE MEASUREMENT TO REDUCE SHELF-STOCKING COSTS

Cases per person-hour have been a good item to track in distributor warehouses and retail stores, particularly grocery stores. I convinced the assistant manager of a small closely held grocery chain to track every delivery over a period of weeks. Productivity ranged from a low of thirty-four cases per person-hour to a high of over sixty cases per person-hour. We recognized immediately that the workers' goals had never been expressed in productivity but rather in survival until the end of the shift. We could see that in filling the schedule, fifteen-hundred-case loads were being done in thirty person-hours at a rate of over fifty cases per person-hour. Several days later a thousand-case load delivered to the same store would require the same number of person-hours—evidence that Dr. Parkinson's laws were indeed at work.

As the crews became aware they were being tracked, productivity picked up. The crews were allowed to go home when the work was finished. And management simply determined that they could pay the crew on a piece-rate basis, which allowed more flexibility in scheduling. Once that was firmly in place, shelf-stocking costs dropped by 27 percent.

AN IDEAL TRACKING SYSTEM FOR NEW SALESPEOPLE

Once I was contacted by a new independent sales agent who was not meeting his sales goals, not even coming close to his expectations. As we discussed the problem, our attention focused on two ideas. One was that if we asked new salespeople to sell one contract their first month and two their second month, we were telling them that they had to double their productivity in one month—their first month, the hardest month of their career. That was no good.

The other idea we kept talking about was something I recalled from a purchasing class in college about a government specification on weapon systems called "mean time between failures." We synthesized the two ideas into what we called MDBS (mean days between sales). We created the following preliminary goals program for new salespeople.

1. Get your first sale as quickly as you can, wherever you can, from whomever you can, for whatever price you can. (We even considered taking a lower price in an effort to give the new salesperson a good closing experience as soon as possible.)

2. Get your second sale in less time than you got the first one.

3. Get your third sale in less than the average of the first two.

4. Continue to beat your average.

After a dismal first ninety days when he was on the verge of resignation, this young man implemented the MDBS tracking system. At the end of a year he was recognized by his company as the national rookie of the year.

This MDBS formula has worked better than any other startup goal-setting process I know of, and it is getting more people into solid sales production in more areas of the country than anything else I know.

The MDBS enables the sales manager to coach salespeople individually. It gives new salespeople a chance to feel the excitement of success through gradual improvement in their production.

IN CONCLUSION

The principles in this book improved performance and increased profitability in nearly every imaginable type of business or organization. These principles are timeless. They work as well in business as they do in athletics and recreation.

Once people are sold on the value of scorekeeping and their personal goals are consistent with the overall goals of the company, with rules clearly defined, and results-to-resources ratios in place, knowing if they are winning or losing every day, their increased productivity will be phenomenal. Being sold is the key, and choice makes the difference. When players help develop their own scorekeeping system, they own it, care for it, and fight to retain it.

When the principles in this book are applied in the workplace, workers will give the same enthusiasm and energy to their work that they give to their recreation. They will enjoy work as much as play, and they will learn how to win at the game of work.

What Is the Game of Work?

Why can ten people with a volleyball and a net achieve teamwork, goal-directed activity, and become a well-managed work team in a matter of minutes at the company picnic, but those same ten people can totally fail to achieve that kind of harmony on the job?

The answer lies in providing the keys to "Enjoying Work as Much as Play." *The Game of Work* examines the phenomenon that people often work harder at sports and athletic endeavors than they do at their jobs. Why? Because in sports a participant has constant feedback on how he or she is doing. The score is known and the effort necessary to win is established. In work, feedback is often unreliable, inconsistent, or nonexistent. The participant seldom knows the score or what it takes to win.

We take the motivation of recreation and apply those winning principles to the workplace to increase profitability and productivity. A small sampling of clients who have implemented these techniques include Pepsi Cola, the U.S. Postal Service, Coca-Cola Consolidated, Dollar General, Associated Grocers, Leslie's Poolmarts, Abbott Labs, Wild Oats, xpedx, the U.S. Air Force, State Farm Insurance, Boeing, American Express, Molina Medical Centers, Coors Brewing, Chicago Tribune, Young Electric Sign Cos., Ralph's Grocery, and General Foods Corporation.

Our money-back guarantee on measurable results achievement provides a no-risk path to higher profitability through increased productivity and employee enthusiasm.

WHAT YOU CAN EXPECT TO LEARN

- *A fresh look at motivation and scorekeeping through:* attitudes of winners—choices— observation—judgments—scorekeeping—implementing a system—turning measurement into a benefit—setting criteria for goals

- *Motivation:* self-evaluation—feedback—types of motivation—coaching

- *Feedback:* graphs and charts—rules and mechanics of scorecards—guidelines for effective feedback

- *Areas of control:* the power of the Results-to-Resources Ratio as a scorekeeping tool

- *How to set up a Results-to-Resources scorekeeping system*

- *Goal setting and motivation*

- *Understanding the Field of Play*

- *Learning how to win every day!*

PROFESSIONAL SERVICES

- Speeches (two-hour, four-hour, or full-day)

- Workshops for your personnel, customers, associations, company meetings, and so on.

- Implementation—a fully customized program of five half-days of specific *Game of Work* implementation with *guaranteed results.*

- Ski & Scheme—three-day executive ski retreat at Deer Valley Resort

For additional information,

call: 1-800-438-6074
or write: The Game of Work
            3100 Pinebrook Road Suite 2500
            Park City, Utah 84098
email: game@gameofwork.com
            www.gameofwork.com

Index

Norman, Greg, 135

O

O'Neal, Shaquille, 133
Odiorne, George, 35
Out-of-Bounds Statement, 82–83

P

Pareto Principle. *See* Eighty-Twenty
    Principle
Parra, Derek, 28
Passion for Excellence, A, 62–63
Perretta, Vinny, 27
Peters, Tom, 62
Phelps, Michael, 16
Profitability, improvement of,
    162–165, 168

R

Rabb, Jerard, 27
Receivables, solving problems with,
    166–168
Repetition, 68–69
Results-to-Resources Ratio: explana-
    tion of, 55–57; in field of play, 80;
    in recreation, 120–121; effectiveness
    in business of, 121; constructing,
    122–125; implementing, 126–131;
    in lumber yard example, 160–161
Return on investment, 119
Rewards, 30–31
Roosevelt, Franklin D., 107
Ruiz, Rosie, 71
Rules: in recreation, 11–13, 71; chang-
    ing of, 75

S

Sanders, Harland, 105–106
Schouman, Derek, 27
Scorekeeping: in recreation, 8–10,
    35–36; as form of motivation, 10;
    must be simple and objective, 46;
    must be self-administered, 46; must
    offer performance comparisons, 47;

should be dynamic, 47; implement-
    ing a system of, 48–49
Singh, Vijay, 135
Spitz, Mark, 136
Strug, Kerri, 101–102
Sutton, Willie, 111

T

Teamwork, 3–4, 33
Tracking system for new salespeople,
    171–172
Twain, Mark, 61

U

Uncertainty, minimization of, 13
Underappreciation, 3

V

Van Andel, Jay, 102

W

Waste, reducing, 169–170
"Why," 30–31
Williams, Ted, 20, 120
Winners: are specific and positive,
    97–98; personal responsibility of,
    98–101; don't seek to change the
    rules, 101–102; willingness to pay the
    price, 102–103; goals of, 103–107;
    are specific, 110–111; understanding
    of probabilities and, 111–118; char-
    acteristics of to look for when hiring,
    134–135. *See also* Winning
Winning: importance of, 93–95;
    preparation for, 95–96; expectations
    of, 96–97; extra effort and,
    135–136
Wooden, John, 2
Woods, Tiger, 96, 103–104
WOW, 80

Z

Zabransky, Jared, 27
Ziglar, Zig, 2

29900074R00109

Made in the USA
San Bernardino, CA
19 March 2019